The Audit Value Factor

Internal Audit and IT Audit

Series Editor:
Dan Swanson, Dan Swanson and Associates, Ltd.,
Winnipeg, Manitoba, Canada

The ***Internal Audit and IT Audit*** series publishes leading-edge books on critical subjects facing audit executives as well as internal and IT audit practitioners. Key topics include Audit Leadership, Cybersecurity, Strategic Risk Management, Auditing Various IT Activities and Processes, Audit Management, and Operational Auditing.

For more information about this series, please visit https://www.crcpress.com/Internal-Audit-and-IT-Audit/book-series/CRCINTAUDITA

The Audit Value Factor
Making Management's Head Turn

Daniel Samson, CIA

CRC Press
Taylor & Francis Group
Boca Raton London New York

CRC Press is an imprint of the
Taylor & Francis Group, an **informa** business

AN AUERBACH BOOK

CRC Press
Taylor & Francis Group
6000 Broken Sound Parkway NW, Suite 300
Boca Raton, FL 33487-2742

© 2020 by Taylor & Francis Group, LLC
CRC Press is an imprint of Taylor & Francis Group, an Informa business

No claim to original U.S. Government works

Printed on acid-free paper

International Standard Book Number-13: 978-1-138-19812-8 (Paperback)

**Visit the Taylor & Francis Web site at
http://www.taylorandfrancis.com**

**and the CRC Press Web site at
http://www.crcpress.com**

Contents

Acknowledgments

There are many people to thank in supporting this effort, not least of which is my spouse Tony Paine. Tony has provided encouragement and patience through countless nights and weekends of writing. A caring partner makes a huge difference.

Effective mentors drive success, and I've been the fortunate beneficiary of outstanding mentoring from some great leaders. Larry Harrington, an inspiring and dedicated champion of the internal audit profession, has provided numerous opportunities and insightful feedback for years. Larry has a passion for people and it shows. He accelerated my career and I'm forever grateful. Dr. Kathryn Bingham, executive coach and founder/CEO of LEADistics provided thoughtful coaching and reassurance through the arduous process of becoming a Six Sigma Black Belt. Kathryn is one of the most decent human beings I know. Dr. Curt Carlson, CEO of Practice of Innovation and the best-selling author of *The Five Disciplines of Innovation*, has provided tremendously helpful disruptive thinking about the profession. I always look forward to our engrossing talks on innovation and sincerely appreciate his ongoing mentorship. Myra Canterbury and Dr. Howard Dockery, entrepreneurs, have brought understanding about the realities of running a business. I thank Richard Chambers, CEO of the Institute of Internal Auditors (IIA), for his time and wisdom and helping us all propel the profession. I also thank the dedicated people working and volunteering at the IIA, who accelerate the value of highly effective internal auditors.

I'm grateful to the following persons: Dr. Aaron Lecklider, the author of *Inventing the Egghead: The Battle over Brainpower in American Culture*, for being a sounding board and for our lifelong friendship; Ann Butera, Barak Engel, Lynn Fountain, fellow authors in this series, who've provided helpful insights; Mark Gibson, CEO of The Next Us, for our many discussions on value propositions; the MIS Training Institute for opportunities to share my story and help other internal auditors deliver value for their customers; Doug Hall, founder of Eureka! Ranch, best-selling author, and serial innovator, for your insights into innovation and creating value; Dan Swanson, editor of the series, for this opportunity; and Richard O'Hanley, publisher at CRC Press, my appreciation.

Author

Daniel Samson is Head of Internal Audit at SRI International, Menlo Park, California, with responsibility for global audit, corporate policies administration, and enterprise risk management. Prior to joining SRI in 2011, he worked as Senior Manager, Internal Audit, and Six Sigma Black Belt at Raytheon Company. He has served on not-for-profit boards in the San Francisco and greater Boston areas and is a former member of the Global Guidance Development Committee for the International Institute of Internal Auditors. Mr. Samson has an undergraduate degree in economics and a graduate degree in administration, and is a Certified Internal Auditor. He is a frequent speaker on auditing for value, process improvement, data analytics, fraud prevention, and risk management.

Mr. Samson can be reached at http://www.linkedin.com/in/danielasamson

INTRODUCTION

The Chief Executive Officer (CEO) of a Fortune 500 company had a major dilemma. Domestic business was flagging from government budget cuts, and the company needed to rapidly accelerate international growth. International business was more stable with higher profit margins, so even a small shift toward international work would balance stagnant domestic sales. The CEO knew that when foreign governments award contracts, they require offsets—investments in domestic industries to spur development. The company decided it needed to assess its offsets strategy to optimize projects, improve value delivered, and reduce risk and cost to achieve its international growth initiative. Each of the company's division presidents were tasked with growing their international segments. Looking around the company, one division leader thought—Who understands process, facilitates change management, articulates and assesses risk, and evaluates controls that I can rely on as a trusted partner? The answer was internal audit. So, the internal audit team led a cross-enterprise project to address the problem, saving an estimated $33 million in cost avoidance, reducing compliance risks, and directly supporting strategic objectives. In other words, internal audit created value. It was one of the most challenging and rewarding efforts during my time at Raytheon. I worked closely with amazing partners across the company from the great leadership team at Raytheon Missile Systems to the President of Raytheon International. The experience solidified my view that internal audit can and must be a value-added strategic partner.

Each of us seeks value in the choices we make. In the case of Raytheon, it was a matter of deciding who could solve an important and urgent problem. If internal audit had a bad track record for delivering value, business leadership may have looked elsewhere for help, perhaps an external consultant. Yet, at Raytheon, internal audit was viewed as an indispensable asset. It had a reputation for driving monumental change. Talent and organizations with that kind of brand will always be in demand.

This book provides methods, ideas, and tools to add value for your customers. The key to remaining relevant is ensuring we consistently deliver value, understand and articulate value propositions, create long-lasting and meaningful customer relationships, develop talent that can deliver value, are the organization's risk expert, facilitate change and process improvement, and provide insights for customers on their data and operations through analytics.

What do internal audit, executive management, the Audit Committee, and individual contributors have in common? Value. Each strives to create and preserve value for the organization. Business leaders want to grow the business, meet customer commitments, and improve profitability. The Audit Committee looks to protect the company's assets has systems in place to monitor risk. Individual contributors strive to meet their goals, have a meaningful impact, and be recognized for their accomplishments. Internal audit looks to determine whether management systems are working effectively and efficiently to support achievement of objectives.

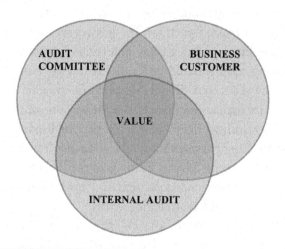

Exhibit Intro 1.0   The common goal is value.

Unfortunately, internal audit's efforts are often lost in translation. We have difficulty explaining our mission. We don't make a strong case for change because we don't speak our customer's language. We struggle to understand what's important because we tend to "tell" instead of "ask." The Audit Value Factor will equip you with the fundamentals and tools to create a value-added internal audit organization, and get management's attention.

Defining Value

Value is in the eye of the beholder, in this case, the customer. Value is something for which customers are willing to pay. Think about your personal situation. When you travel on a plane, do you value early boarding, having extra legroom, checking your bag, having a meal during the flight? These are all things for which customers, in some instances, are willing to pay extra because they derive value. The à la carte pricing by airlines is certainly not popular, but the industry understands what customers value.

Value can be better quality service, convenience, and responsiveness. It can also be benefits derived from an internal audit effort, such as an optimized control structure, which requires less person hours to support, or a reduction in operating costs because a process is not lean. It can mean a clearer and distilled understanding of risks for the leadership team and the Audit Committee. Or it could mean deep insights into the company's own data, creating ah-ha moments for stakeholders.

Dr. Curt Carlson, author of *The Five Disciplines of Innovation*, laid out a vision for value. He said value is defined by our customers. People tend to focus on the benefits associated with value but forget the other side of the ledger—costs. Achieving value requires investment of resources such as people and capital. In his book, Dr. Carlson proposes that potential projects be ranked based on a value factor:

$$\text{Value Factor} = \text{Perceived Benefits}/\text{Perceived Costs}$$

Extending this concept, we can assess audit recommendations based on value. Doing so builds a stronger case for why recommendations should be accepted.

For example, consider a process that has weak controls to comply with a regulation. In conjunction with the internal customer, assess the cost of noncompliance. For example, if noncompliance could result in fines and penalties of $500,000, civil suits of $1,000,000, and loss of revenue of $5,000,000, total perceived benefits would be $6,500,000. Now consider the same for perceived cost. If perceived costs of implementing a solution to comply, for example, information system changes, are $100,000, the value factor would be calculated as follows:

$$\text{Value Factor} = \$6,500,000/\$100,000 = 65$$

In this example, the benefit covers the cost by a factor of 65.

The same can be done to determine whether an operational audit is worthwhile. For example, consider an assessment of an administrative function that has $10,000,000 in annual operating costs. If we are able to identify a 10% savings by assessing workflows for efficiency, that equates with $1,000,000 in benefits. Now consider that the consulting project requires 1,000 hours of personnel time at $50/h or $50,000, plus an additional $50,000 in labor to implement recommendations, for a total cost of $100,000. The value factor would be calculated as follows:

$$\text{Value Factor} = \$1,000,000/\$100,000 = 10$$

In this example, the benefit covers the cost by a factor of 10.

So long as benefits outweigh costs, we can make a strong case for change. The customer actively participated in the process and we have buy-in! This concept can be applied to every internal audit recommendation and proposed project.

How do internal auditors know whether they are adding value? Another way of thinking about this is by asking a few simple questions.

- Is the customer willing to pay for audits?
- Is the customer cheering for audit's participation on projects?
- Does the customer call internal audit when a significant problem arises?
- Has internal audit been involved in change that had a positive impact?

Every audit or project must have a value-added outcome for the customer. If the customer doesn't perceive value from the engagement, internal audit has failed. Customer perceptions of value are linked to not only outcomes but also the relationship that has been developed or not developed with that customer. If strong customer relationships have not been developed before the audit commences, it's more likely that we won't understand what's of value. There is also the possibility that an audit team does a great job completing a project on time with the expected deliverables, but poor communication overshadows the positive results. We discuss the importance of communication in the Customer Relationship Factor.

Asking the audit customer about the benefits and costs of change helps us understand how valuable the change is and whether it is worth pursuing. This value factor can be estimated before a project begins. If the Audit Value Factor (AVF) is less than 1.0, the cost outweighs the benefit and should be carefully considered before moving forward. If the AVF is 1.0, the benefits and costs are equal and may not warrant an investment. If the AVF is greater than 1.0, there is greater justification for the project.

This analysis also helps internal audit optimize the use of its resources. Comparing the AVF of various potential projects helps prioritize those with the highest value. There will always be varying viewpoints on perceived benefits and costs; however, this is a systematic way to prioritize projects. Perceived benefits and costs are projections that may differ from actual benefits and costs.

How much value did you deliver last year, last month, last week? Can that question be answered? How will you remain relevant in a fast-changing world? It is incumbent upon each of us to recognize our present circumstances and take charge of our future. Too often professionals, internal auditors included, become complacent. We check-the-box on our careers, doing just enough to get by. Meanwhile, the rest of the world is eager. If we want to own our destiny, we need to make a concerted, conscious effort to be innovative and deliver value for our customers. Think of yourself as an LLC. If LLC A delivers value timelier, more efficiently, and more effectively, it's bound to see greater rewards than LLC B, which doesn't understand the customer's wants, have the talent to deliver value, or have the ability to communicate for success.

In Silicon Valley, we see the acceleration of the gig economy, where workers market their skills for short projects at various companies. Gig artists that deliver value are in demand. It's not uncommon for a professional in the Valley to change companies after 6 months. In fact, many seek job moves and are rewarded with significant pay increases for each jump. Others are self-employed for greater flexibility. In both scenarios, many of these professionals have side projects, where they own the intellectual property and look to launch their own start-ups. On the weekends, they self-teach new computer languages, maintain their personal websites and blogs, and tinker with a new application they're developing. All of these efforts create more opportunities and security because *they* are in charge. They are passionate about their trade.

Why should internal auditors care about Silicon Valley professionals? Because the gig economy is coming to everyone. If we are unable to articulate and deliver value, someone else will. I'm a big believer in firms that provide co-sourcing services, supplementing skills, and providing thought leadership. They can also be a threat to an underperforming internal audit function that is unable to change and meet company and customer needs. Likewise, artificial intelligence and automation are rapidly changing how we do business and live our lives. No job, company, or person is immune from imminent technological change. The elimination and creation of jobs and whole professions by artificial intelligence and automation are well under way.

Consider the last time you used a travel agent or telephone operator. The operator transferred calls seamlessly. The travel agent reserved your desired flight with a stay at your preferred hotel. Yet it didn't matter. Technology turned phones into computers with more processing power than government computers from the 1980s. Those same mini computers were then used to search and book travel in the palm of our hands, at our leisure, not during dictated office hours of a travel agency. Those jobs were no longer needed and non-value added. Artificial intelligence and automation shifted the paradigm.

What about the self-checkout at the supermarket. The cashier, previously in that role, was efficient and knowledgeable about completing a transaction. They acted as a gatekeeper to make sure customers paid before leaving the store. Now we scan and bag our own groceries, sensors determining that each item has been accounted for, and we can pay with our phones or watches.

Now massive change has come to the taxi industry. The gig economy created jobs for people to earn extra cash working for Uber or Lyft, generating revenue using their cars. In 2010, traditional yellow cab drivers saw no threat to their safe, reliable jobs. Then Uber and subsequently Lyft were created. The number of taxi trips has plummeted by 65% in San Francisco. Technology effectively eliminated the middleman (dispatch and taxi administration) and corresponding city regulations. Now anyone can be a cab driver. In fact, there are upwards of 45,000 Uber and Lyft drivers in San Francisco. The same thing is unfolding in major cities around the world. And yet, automation will upend the industry again. All of those Uber and Lyft drivers will be out of work in the near future, once cars are autonomous. The same is true for the trucking industry, which is expected to be the first to adopt driverless vehicles. In April 2016, a caravan of driverless trucks made a cross border trip arriving in the Netherlands[1]. According to the American Trucking Association, 3.5 million Americans drive a truck for a living.

The dream of a manufacturing renaissance ignores the reality that artificial intelligence and automation are the root cause for industrial workforce declines. Manufacturing jobs will only further diminish with the advancement of 3D printing capabilities, which will enable custom, on-demand, in-home production for all your needs.

It's not just blue-collar jobs. Stockbrokers have been displaced by online trading. Real estate agents are competing with an abundance of freely available data and connected tools. Soon doctors, nurses, and healthcare professionals will face artificial intelligence and robotic augmentation, substantially changing their professions. SRI International recently launched a company called Superflex, which enables people with mobility challenges to live more independently, potentially allowing greater independent living.

Internal audit is not immune from these developments. According to the World Economic Forum's 2015 Technological Tipping Points Survey, 30% of audits will be performed by artificial intelligence by 2025. Who among us believes that current practices will meet customer needs 10 years from now? Each of us must act now to proactively anticipate and address future customer needs. We need to embrace and leverage technology and ensure that our work is focused on customer value.

Traditionally, the audit profession has focused on assurance services. The Institute of Internal Auditors defines assurance services as "an objective examination of evidence to provide an independent assessment of governance, risk management, and control processes for the organization." Expectations for the profession continue to evolve, while simultaneously internal audit staffing stagnates or grows slower than the complexity of the organizations that we serve.

Value must be at the core of the internal audit organization's mission, methods, and goals. Value requires having a systematic approach to planning, executing, and ultimately achieving value-add during every engagement.

Getting Started

Before charging ahead, we need to understand the expectations of our primary stakeholders; namely the Audit Committee and executive team. To better understand your mandate, consider the following:

- Does the internal audit charter include provisions for consulting services, sometimes noted as management requests? If so, it's more likely that the management team and Audit Committee have a better understanding of the topic.
- What is the history of the internal audit organization? Is this a new group or existing? If internal audit is established, examine prior audit plans for consulting engagements. If stand-alone consulting engagements have not been performed, seek information as to why. If consulting engagements have been conducted, this is a good indication that the Audit Committee and executive leadership team are open to the concept, and therefore, less socialization may be necessary for these types of engagements.
- What is most critical to the executive team? Meet with them to understand their needs. Do they reference structural and process inefficiencies, excessive cost of operations, or budgetary pressures? All of these may be indicative of opportunities to add value.
- What are the CEO's strategic objectives for the enterprise?
- Which stakeholders in the organization carry significant influence? Ask what is important to them. Query about the history of the company and their experiences with internal audit. Have they partnered with internal audit previously? Was it a good experience? Positive prior experiences will help pave the way for further partnership.

Traditional assurance services are the foundation and primary mission for most internal audit organizations. Having a sense of balance is important when incorporating consulting work within the audit plan. Consider setting aside 25% of total audit hours specifically for special projects, management requests, and consulting engagements. I recently conducted a survey related to articulating value in conjunction with the Institute of Internal Auditors Audit Executive Center. The survey received responses from 150 Chief Audit Executives. Seventy-one percent of respondents dedicated less than 20% of their audit plan to consulting-type projects. Forty-three percent of respondents indicated that they frequently include a consulting component during assurance/audit engagements. Seventy-one percent did not measure value provided to management through quantitative methods. For those that did quantitatively measure value, 61% used customer surveys, 42% measured cost savings in dollars, 40% measured cost avoidance in dollars, 35% cited the number of controls improved, 35% measured revenue recovery in dollars, 33% stated number of findings, and 33% said the number of major risks mitigated. Note that respondents could chose all that applied. The survey showed an opportunity for internal audit organizations to focus on value delivery and articulating value provided.

The number of hours devoted to consulting engagements will vary based on executive leadership and Audit Committee preference and whether we have made a compelling case for such efforts.

The question remains, are we able to make these projects optimal and have we articulated the value provided?

If the company has not enculturated consulting engagements, starting slowly with a pilot effort can be an effective approach, enabling stakeholders within the enterprise to see the benefits of such projects. Seek internal stakeholders with pressing operational needs and limited staffing.

I have successfully partnered with leaders of supply chain organizations over the years, resulting in tens of millions of dollars in savings. Supply chain organizations typically have three primary objectives: fulfilling customer requirements efficiently, preventing disruptions of critical customer needs, and optimizing cost. Each of these objectives aligns well with internal audit's skills.

Another natural pilot partner is the finance organization. Here the alignment is supporting the Chief Financial Officer's objectives to optimize the cost and control environment, which can include process efficiencies. Too often, internal audit recommendations are associated with adding steps to a process instead of optimizing it. Internal auditors often feel they provide value by recommending new controls, when in fact, value can be created by optimizing the existing control structure and eliminating duplicative processes and controls. When was the last time you or your team recommended removing a duplicative control?

The CEO can be an excellent initial partner, given their purview of the entire enterprise. Working initially with the CEO raises the stature of internal audit, establishing branding, and sends a signal that if internal audit is competent enough to deliver value for the CEO, it is sufficiently qualified to provide value to other leaders. The CEO will also have significant influence in creating support for these efforts with the Audit Committee. A word of caution; a poor initial showing with the CEO could result in the opposite outcome.

Conducting a roadshow about internal audit's mission and objectives and highlighting service offerings can be a great way to build support. There are a multitude of opportunities at every company by just asking the rank and file; particularly employees working at regional offices, where their experiences and perceptions may be quite different from headquarters. There is little downside to creating awareness that internal audit also has consulting-related objectives. We've all had countless individuals over the years recount negative experiences with internal auditors, who didn't take the time to listen actively and understand their needs. Each of us has been guilty of driving these perceptions at one time or another.

The Audit Committee, internal audit's primary customer, cannot be overlooked when building the case for adding value. The Audit Committee's main objective is to monitor the effectiveness of management systems on financial reporting, internal control, risk management, and compliance. However, if we consider who sits on Audit Committees, we can appreciate their interest in operational excellence. Many Audit Committee members are former CEOs, CFOs, business owners, and leaders in their respective areas of expertise, such as supply chain management and information systems. While consulting engagements will likely remain a secondary priority for

Audit Committee members concerning the audit plan, many of them understand the positive, meta impact that internal audit can have on an organization when it is helping to improve processes, reduce cost, and assist internal customers in meeting their goals and objectives. Value-centric engagements ultimately help build the relationships, confidence, and trust needed to improve the overall efficacy of the internal audit function. Introducing this concept early in a newly formed internal audit function, therefore, is essential.

This book is not intended to diminish the importance of foundational principles; rather, the goal is to bolster our capabilities to deliver value. At the end of each chapter, there is a summary of key points for seamless use. Throughout the book tools are denoted by ✘.

Bibliography

American Trucking Association, www.trucking.org/News_and_Information_ Reports_Industry_Data.aspx.

Dr. Curtis R. Carlson and William W. Wilmot, The Five Disciplines of Innovation, 2006, Crown Business.

The Guardian, "Convoy of self-driving trucks completes first European cross-border trip", April 7, 2016.

Institute of Internal Auditors, Audit Executive Center.

www.sfgate.com/bayarea/article/Taxi-use-plummets-in-San-Francisco-65-percent-in-5760251.php.

World Economic Forum 2015 Technological Tipping Points Survey, www3. weforum.org/docs/WEF_GAC15_Technological_Tipping_Points_ report_2015.pdf.

FACTOR 1
VALUE PROPOSITIONS

Lyft, the ride sharing company, has a simple value proposition, "Rides in Minutes." It addresses an urgent need—getting a ride, communicates a benefit—quick service, and differentiates itself from the competition (taxis) with an emphasis on convenience. It conveys everything you need to know in three words. Gusto, another San Francisco company, has a value proposition reflecting the effortlessness of using its services: "The easiest way to pay your employees." Gusto provides payroll services. Dollar Shave Club, a direct delivery razor blade provider's value proposition is "Get Ready to Look, Feel, and Smell your Best." Value propositions summarize why an organization's product or service is the preferred choice for a customer. Inherent in a value proposition is providing greater value than the competition offers; a value differentiator.

How does this apply to internal audit? Well, it actually applies to all goods and services. Everyone makes choices about resource allocations based on perceived value. When buying a car, people consider: economy, style, special features, quality, acceleration, color, size, whether it's two-wheel or four-wheel drive, whether it's a domestic or foreign make, and last but not least, affordability. There is also the intangible factor that makes us decide we want *that* car. A company allocating budgets is no different. Corporate functions are regularly viewed as compulsory overhead costs. It's become tempting to outsource services such as human resources, information technology, aspects of accounting and finance, facilities management, supply chain, legal, and internal audit. There is also the continued advancement of automation and artificial/augmented intelligence to contend with. Understanding customer needs, proactively addressing the competition, and articulating organizational value is key to remaining relevant and sought-after. Developing a value proposition helps position this success.

SRI International's value proposition is "We invent products and solutions that change the world." SRI is an independent, nonprofit research center. It invents solutions for the most challenging problems today and in the future. For more than 70 years, SRI has led the discovery and design of groundbreaking products, technologies, and industries—from Siri and online banking to medical ultrasound, cancer treatments, and much more. SRI is a diverse business addressing multiple customers and industries. A significant percentage of its funding comes from the federal government, which brings substantial regulatory requirements. It also works with commercial and international customers to innovate products and services. Imagine for a moment a value proposition for SRI's internal audit organization. It has to embrace the customer need—innovation, articulate the value provided, and differentiate from the competition. SRI Internal Audit decided on a value proposition of "Empowering High Value Innovations and Solutions." We use this to market our services and to keep the team focused on customer value. It flows through all that we do. Internal audit team members have specific goals associated with delivering value and customer satisfaction. We layout our vision through our value proposition and then measure our performance in delivering value.

Raytheon Company's value proposition is "Customer Success is Our Mission." Raytheon is a technology and innovation leader specializing in defense, civil, and cybersecurity markets throughout the world. When Larry Harrington was brought in about 15 years ago, the internal audit function had been outsourced with mixed results. Audits and projects were not being completed timely, and there were delays in communicating results to management. Larry had successfully reinvented internal audit organizations twice before at Staples and Aetna Health. He saw an opportunity to rebrand internal audit and disrupt prior perceptions. Larry's value proposition was "Creating Positive Change with a Sense of Urgency." It perfectly captured the customer's need for value—creating positive change, with the need for speed which was a core theme at Raytheon. Understanding the prior outsourced experience, it also stressed that the internal audit organization was better than the competition. His internal audit organization would deliver on or ahead of time. Everyone within the team was committed to this value proposition. It became our philosophy.

External service providers, internal audit's main competition, have mastered the art of the pitch and value propositions. Value is the central theme in their sales presentations. They do extensive research to prepare marketing materials. This includes sending annual surveys to board of director members, CEOs and CFOs, and internal audit leaders. They ask about top risk concerns, assess whether internal audit is addressing the interests of management and adding value, and whether competent services are being delivered. They package the survey results into white papers, such as PwC's "State of the Internal Audit Profession." It's brilliant. These external service providers are framing the conversation for management and the board about what they need, on their terms. In turn, they shape their offerings to address the perceived gaps in value being delivered.

Meanwhile, the typical internal audit organization is playing catchup and not driving the conversation about value. The result is a near constant perception that internal audit is falling behind. To remain relevant, we need to take the helm and proactively identify what customers perceive as value-added. I know, I know, we have all asked the question "what keeps you up at night?" Maybe we're asking the wrong question or collecting the wrong data. Every 2–3 years I send a survey to all of my customers—every employee in the company. One of the questions I typically ask is "If one thing could change to make your job easier, what would it be?" You'd be amazed at the feedback and appreciation for the question. The information being sought is customer and value-centric. It's about what would help *them* (value) in *their* own words. We're not asking how *internal audit* can help them. That's a different question and quickly narrows the thought process. The average employee won't know how *internal audit* can help. The data create ah-ha moments for management. Everyone is focused on execution; we don't step back and ask what would make it easier for employees to accomplish their objectives. Using this survey technique—internal audit is now adding value by providing the executive team with new information, and in turn, crafting an audit plan that addresses some of those needs. External service providers would love to have that information!

We are the only ones holding ourselves back from having well-founded value propositions and understanding what's important to our customers.

Developing a Value Proposition for Internal Audit

It was my first interview with Dr. Curt Carlson, the former CEO of SRI International. I was in London on vacation with family, and we video conferenced about the opportunity to innovate internal audit at SRI. Internal audit had a reputation of being punitive, and Dr. Carlson was looking for a major change in vision. Interestingly, during the 45 minutes we chatted, the mechanics of internal audit barely came up. Instead, we extensively discussed the importance of innovation and value, and how successful organizations operate. It was refreshing. SRI wanted to innovate all of its corporate functions to better align with its mission. My next several interviews were with business presidents—the leaders at SRI responsible for empowering its researchers to innovate. Again, the discussions focused on how internal audit could deliver value for the organization. By this time, I had a keen awareness about the criticality of innovation for the company.

One of the first things I did when I joined the company was to better understand the current state of internal audit's brand. I met with the leaders of every business and function, attended town halls to speak with employees, visited regional offices, and met one-on-one with laboratory directors and researchers. I listened. A lot. My first question was simple. What do you think of internal audit? Some people weren't aware of internal audit's purpose. Others had negative views. The one theme that consistently came through was one of constraint. There was a perception that internal audit was at the company to constrain innovation and collaboration because it was focused on compliance. In other words—internal audit's brand was the polar opposite of the company's value proposition and mission. Significant change was needed. I followed basic system theory: inputs, process, and outputs. Inputs are the data and information needed to understand the current state and customer expectations for what a value-added internal audit organization looked like. Process was the infrastructure to enact the change required. Outputs represented the tangible changes and the types of services to be offered by internal audit.

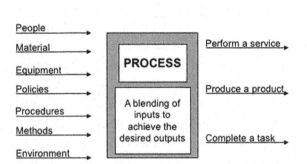

INPUTS   OUTPUTS

People

Material   Perform a service

Equipment   **PROCESS**

Policies   Produce a product

Procedures   A blending of
                   inputs to
Methods   achieve the
                   desired outputs   Complete a task

Environment

Exhibit 1.1 Inputs, Process, Outputs.

I evaluated internal audit's current practices (inputs) and found that there was no methodology, charter, mission statement, performance metrics, or customer feedback loop. No wonder the audit organization was unsuccessful. The prior internal audit organization viewed itself as a necessity, not a source of value for the company. We looked at the company's strategic plan, goals, and objectives (inputs). We asked customers about their past interactions with the internal audit team. The general perception was that internal audit did a lot of "telling" and not too much "asking." The final set of inputs was asking about the ideal state. What would the ideal internal audit organization look like? Note that a side benefit of this exercise was raising awareness about internal audit and possibilities for customers. We evaluated all of the inputs and created meaningful outputs as a result of the evaluation.

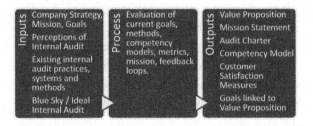

Inputs	Process	Outputs
Company Strategy, Mission, Goals	Evaluation of current goals, methods, competency models, metrics, mission, feedback loops.	Value Proposition
Perceptions of Internal Audit		Mission Statement
Existing internal audit practices, systems and methods		Audit Charter
Blue Sky / Ideal Internal Audit		Competency Model
		Customer Satisfaction Measures
		Goals linked to Value Proposition

Exhibit 1.2 Example of Inputs, Process, Outputs for value proposition development.

The last step in developing the value proposition was market testing. I wanted the value proposition to shock the system and radically challenge the prior perception of internal audit. We asked customers what they thought about "Empowering High Value Innovations and Solutions." They loved it! It drove home a new commitment to customer success and value. About 12 months later, I noticed something interesting. The new CIO had adopted our value proposition. As Oscar Wilde wrote, imitation is the sincerest form of flattery.

Going back to Dr. Carlson—he and Dr. Bill Wilmot outlined a value proposition model called NABC (Need, Approach, Benefits per costs, and Competition) in their excellent book *The Five Disciplines of Innovation*. Dr.'s Carlson and Wilmot believed that everyone has customers, and we need to understand the various aspects of value for each of them in order to advance the enterprise's success. This starts with understanding the customer's need: what is the important customer and market need? Development continues with approach: what is the unique approach for addressing this need? The B represents benefits: what are the specific benefits per costs that result from the approach? Lastly, consider the competition: how are these benefits per costs superior to the competition and the alternatives?[1] Surely, there was an opportunity for internal audit to leverage this approach in our work.

Value Propositions for Individual Audits

First and foremost, what is the *need* for the audit or project in terms that relate to the customer's goals and objectives? Why should they care? The audit may be on the audit plan as a result of the company's risk assessment—perhaps an urgent or emerging risk or developing regulatory requirement—justifies looking at a particular process or set of controls. It's important to connect that justification to the customer's own interests. How does it relate to the customer's goals, objectives, and strategic plan? Translate the need in customer terms. Having a meaningful value proposition for every audit or project creates buy-in and engagement. Typically, internal audit relies on the enterprise risk assessment or audit plan to justify an audit, yet that may not articulate value for the customer. A value proposition describes how an audit will solve an important problem and benefit the customer.

For example, an audit of information security was included in the audit plan because the cyber threat to the company is constantly evolving and the executive team needs assurance that the program is effective at addressing cyber risks. A value proposition for the executive team and the Chief Information Security Officer (CISO) could be "Internal Audit will provide assurance about whether the information security program can support customer growth of 25% over the next 24 months." This example takes the typical audit objective and links to the company's strategic goals. Now value is evident. Ideally value propositions are developed *before* an audit is added to the audit plan. Each proposed audit or project should be evaluated for its contribution toward supporting strategic goals and objectives as relates to risk management. Some additional examples of value propositions:

Example—Sarbanes–Oxley Controls

Traditional Objective Statement: "Verify that controls are effective and efficient to comply with Sarbanes–Oxley regulatory requirements."

Value Proposition Statement: "Assess Sarbanes–Oxley controls in preparation for the Company's initial public offering."

We could easily substitute the "initial public offering" with whatever the current strategic plan reflects—perhaps its growth, a planned acquisition or merger, or cost optimization effort. The key point is that internal audit is not simply justifying the audit on the grounds of an existing regulatory requirement—we are illustrating value to the customer beyond compliance and approaching the audit with the expectation of value-added deliverables. We're contributing to the company's ability to go public, engage in merger activity, or optimize the cost environment. Internal audit is creating value for its customer.

Example—Business Continuity

Traditional Objective Statement: "Verify that controls are effective and efficient to support continuation of operations in the event of an incident or disaster."

Value Proposition Statement: "Assess business continuity practices in support of expansion to Asia."

The objectives are linked to the strategic plan, so value is immediately evident to the customer. The audit becomes more strategic, is forward looking, and is more valuable. Here again, "expansion of operations to Asia" could be substituted for whatever priority is outlined in the company's strategic plan.

You may be saying—well, I don't have access to the company's strategic plan and therefore, I'm unable to create a meaningful value proposition. Gaining access to the company's strategic goals may not come in the form of attendance at the CEO's staff meeting, strategic planning meetings, or other high-level executive planning sessions. Depending on company culture, this information may need to be cultivated through other avenues, where a customer relationship has been established and information is willingly shared. Ultimately, hearing firsthand about company strategy is ideal, but there are other means for achieving this objective. Attend company All-Hands meetings. Seek out and develop mentoring relationships with key members of management. Ask for personal briefings on the organization's strategy. Information will also flow once trust has been established as discussed earlier in the chapter.

How we approach the audit is equally important. What specific value-added deliverables will be provided to the customer during the review? Without thoughtful planning, audits may focus entirely on answering questions about compliance or the effectiveness of controls. Every engagement should provide "ah-ha" moments and golden nuggets for the customer. Dr. Carlson described golden nuggets as a key to success that might be in the form of "a new, enabling technology, a relationship, a novel manufacturing process, or a new business model." When we think about value for customers, we need to determine how we will differentiate ourselves from an external provider or other internal or external resource. Dr. Carlson continues, "As in panning for gold, you are always looking for something extremely valuable that others don't have and your customers want."[15] Golden nuggets for audit customers may come in the form of recommendations to optimize cost or increase revenue. For example, performing a process analysis using the SMART system, described in the Change Management and Process Optimization Factor, could reveal low-value activities, duplicative controls, or ways the customer can better meet objectives. Golden nuggets could be provided by enabling customers to better understand their business through data analytics. Benchmark information regarding industry and peer company practices provide valuable insights too. Each of these examples necessitates conscious planning and setting expectations for the audit team early in the audit process.

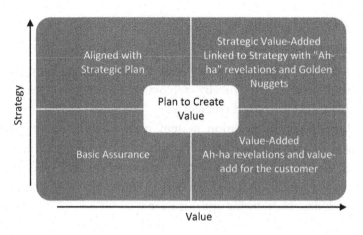

Exhibit 1.3 Value proposition quadrant.

The following are examples of basic assurance, strategic, value-added, and strategic value-added approaches to value propositions.

Basic Assurance

Basic assurance, a given, is the minimal expectation of any audit or project. Internal audit organizations with a primary goal of providing basic assurance are more traditional in nature, tend to be less agile, and may not prioritize customer value. Examples of basic assurance include

- Validating that current Sarbanes–Oxley controls are working as intended.
- Verifying that information system access is appropriate given user roles and responsibilities.

Aligned with Strategic Plan

- Validating that the Sarbanes–Oxley Program has an effective risk assessment and change management program to respond to changes in business operations and that the design of controls addresses changes in organization strategy.
- Verifying that the information system roadmap considers and is responsive to the organization's strategic plan.

Value–Added

- Assessing whether certain Sarbanes–Oxley controls can be automated via Robotic Process Automation or Augmented Intelligence, and thereby deploying organization resources more effectively and efficiently.
- Identifying information system users that never or rarely access system resources, access the system at unusual times, or access system information that is unexpected. Identify users that generate computer processing time that is not aligned with expectations for optimization.

Strategic Value–Added

- Verifying that the Sarbanes–Oxley Program has a roadmap to address the strategic plan and optimize the use of resources via Robotic Process Automation or Augmented Intelligence. Assess the program's efficiency as relates to external benchmarks and make recommendations.
- Verifying that the information systems roadmap is aligned with the organization's strategic plan and that resources are deployed efficiently. Recommend where Robotic Process Automation or Augmented Intelligence could be deployed to further optimize the use of resources given strategic plan objectives.

With ideal engagement, we move up and to the right in the value proposition quadrant. The goal should always be to move toward more strategic and value-added engagement with the customer. We must be agile and responsive to changing needs to remain relevant and add value. The Change Management and Process Optimization Factor includes many tools to help achieve a value-added approach to audit work.

The benefits per costs associated with audits and audit recommendations are often overlooked. Going back to the Audit Executive Center Survey discussed in the introduction, 71% of Chief Audit Executives did not measure value provided to management through quantitative methods. How can we expect management to understand the value provided by internal audit, if we aren't telling the story? It's imperative that we quantify benefits provided during every engagement. We also need to provide a full accounting of costs too. Audit recommendations tend to be cost additive because new or enhanced controls are being recommended. Helping management understand the net benefit of a change drives buy-in. Make it as easy for customers to understand your value proposition in all that you do.

The last item that Dr. Carlson and Wilmot discussed was competition. What are the alternative solutions (competition) to performing the audit. The company could pull together a cross-sectional project team or hire an external consultant. Maybe there's another group within the company that does special projects. What makes internal audit stand out as the best option and how do you convey that to the customer? For starters, internal audit brings extensive experience in change management, it's a multidisciplinary team, has unfettered access to resources and information, and has a broad understanding of the entire enterprise. I would argue that internal audit is better positioned than most other functional teams to help solve important problems and deliver tangible value. The competition aspect for internal audit is not necessarily about spelling out how much a consultant would charge to perform similar work, it's really about anticipating what a consultant, alternative inside team, or external service provider can offer and building a better proposal, taking those factors into account. Internal audit will almost always be a better value based on pricing (cost). The value proposition for an audit or project should proactively address gaps in knowledge or expertise by bringing in specialized resources to supplement the team. I've often brought in subject-matter experts from external service providers to provide extra technical knowledge. Doing so demonstrates sophistication and willingness to bring the best resources available to increase the likelihood of a value-added outcome.

Chapter Recap

Value propositions increase the likelihood that your organization will remain relevant and thrive. Value propositions should be linked directly to customer needs. The internal audit value proposition should be aligned and responsive to the company's value proposition and strategic objectives. An effective value proposition succinctly differentiates internal audit from the competition. Value propositions should also be developed for individual audits to communicate, from the customer's point of view, why an audit is important to them. They should consider customer strategic objectives and how value will be delivered. Identifying a value proposition for individual audits sets an expectation for audit team members about the value to be delivered at the completion of the audit. Strive to move up and to the right in the value proposition quadrant.

Notes

1 Dr. Curtis R. Carlson and William W. Wilmot, The Five Disciplines of Innovation, page 88, 145. Crown Business, 2006.

Bibliography

Dr. Curtis R. Carlson and Dr. William W. Wilmot, The Five Disciplines of Innovation, 2006, Crown Business.
https://gusto.com.
www.dollarshaveclub.com.
www.lyft.com.
www.raytheon.com.
www.sri.com.

FACTOR 2
CUSTOMER RELATIONSHIPS

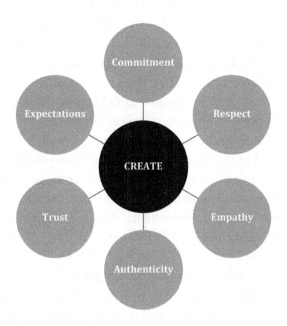

Mark, an ambitious, early career auditor, had a reputation for getting projects done quickly. He is auditing the company's Philippines operation and plans to complete the review in two weeks. Lindsey, the Controller in Manila, is eager to support a smooth review but hasn't worked with Mark before and was notified about the audit yesterday. She is working on special projects for the operation's President and is concerned the review may interfere with existing commitments. Mark emailed Lindsey a list of documents in the morning with a 24 hour turnaround time; he wants to review the documents before boarding his flight. Lindsey was surprised to receive a request for documents at 9 PM Manila time, and it was unclear from the request, which documents Mark needed. Later that evening, she emailed Mark the data she could find and sent a list of questions for the remaining items before going to bed. Mark didn't reply until noon the next day, midnight Manila time. The remaining documents never made it to Mark before departing for the Philippines, and Lindsey was already exhausted and frustrated.

While on the flight, Mark contemplated yet another successful audit. He expected to find many issues because the operation hadn't been reviewed in several years and was excited about the recognition he'd receive at corporate headquarters. He fell asleep while reading.

Dreams set in. The controller thanked him when he arrived for reaching out to her several months in advance. Their conversations were easy, since they frequently met for lunch during her visits to corporate headquarters. Lindsey liked that Mark provided a list of processes to be audited in advance to facilitate a self-assessment and that he recommended ways to improve controls based on best practices. He had also connected her with the controllers in the United Kingdom and Hong Kong. The pre-visit data analysis completed by internal audit helped to identify cost reduction opportunities. The next two weeks were productive because internal audit focused on validating the control improvements already implemented. It really felt like Mark was committed to Lindsey's success.

Mark awakened with a jolt, realizing that it was all a dream and he had not developed a positive relationship with the customer.

Auditors are task oriented. We check the box and get stuff done—completing the audit program and issuing the report while planning for the next project. Lost in the effort is our impact on customers. We create a whirlwind: requesting information, conducting interviews, and going back with additional information requests, sometimes multiple times in a day. We reassure them that the intense activity will be short-lived. The relationship is a transaction; we ask—they give. Unfortunately, we lose a valuable opportunity with this method. The customer is less likely to approach us with a problem, ask for advice, or include us in initiatives, all of which diminishes opportunities to add value. There is value in creating long-lasting and meaningful customer relationships that transcend individual audits and projects. The following outlines a framework to achieve that goal. We need to commit to the customer, develop mutual respect, embody empathy and authenticity in our interactions, cultivate trust, and proactively and continuously engage with them, and understand expectations.

Commitment

How do you demonstrate commitment to customer success? Independence and objectivity are critical pillars of internal audit; yet, they don't preclude commitment and dedication to customers. Audit work often feels like something we do to our customers, not for our customers. The mind-set is frequently centered on finding issues, which becomes obvious during interactions. Our work is completed and the results are communicated, but do we follow up to see how the implementation of changes is going? Perhaps some of the recommendations resulted in unintended negative consequences. Following up several weeks and months after an audit is complete, demonstrates commitment to the customer's long-term success, and provides opportunities to deliver additional value.

In Mark's case, he lost an opportunity to develop a relationship with the customer before the audit. Had he met Lindsey for lunch while she visited corporate headquarters, they could have discussed operational challenges. Mark would have an opening to deliver value early by sharing best practices or making efforts to position Lindsey for a successful outcome. At the end of the day, the goal is improved internal controls and reduced risk, not to identify issues. Developing a relationship ahead of an audit mitigates risk sooner and sets the table for a non-adversarial relationship.

Everyone Needs to Eat

Take your customer to lunch or coffee. It can be challenging to find time during busy schedules to meet for the sake of relationship building. Customer time is precious and should be respected. Yet, everyone needs to eat, and having a meal together is an effective icebreaker. Casual discussions help take the temperature of the company. What issues have teams encountered with a new system or policy? Conversations reveal where risk or issues might emerge for later consideration. Having lunch with customers forms bonds. It builds familiarity. The physical barriers of an office, such as a desk or a conference table, are eliminated. Breaking bread can ease future tensions. As Oscar Wilde said, "After a good dinner one can forgive anybody, even one's own relatives."

Do You Hear What I Hear?

Use active listening to understand customer obstacles. Active listening means being present and attentively listening to what someone is saying without distraction. We all struggle for various reasons with listening. Put away mobile devices to lessen interference. Look at your customer while they're speaking. Position your body to demonstrate engagement. Unfold your arms. Unclasp your hands. Don't interrupt. Avoid excessive facial expressions, which can be a distraction. The focus is listening to understand. Modify your approach based on visual cues. As Stephen R. Covey said, "Most people do not listen with the intent to understand; they listen with the intent to reply."

Give Back

Volunteering for a company event together creates common bonds and interests. Common bonds develop a mutual commitment to success. It's much harder to have an adversarial relationship with someone that shares your interests. Challenges are more easily overcome because both people understand there is a broader relationship at stake. The extra time together builds understanding. We've all heard someone say something along the lines of "oh that's just Bob." Bob may be joking, but his dry sense of humor is misunderstood because we aren't familiar with Bob's style. Volunteering shines a light on how people solve problems. Is your customer team oriented? There is also the benefit of doing something for a worthy cause together. You have an affirmative impact for the charity and the customer. The great Maya Angelou said, "I've learned that you shouldn't go through life with a catcher's mitt on both hands. You need to be able to throw something back."

Grow Your Garden

Just like gardening, customer relationships need nurturing and attention. It takes time and consistency to yield healthy bonds. Waiting until an audit to engage a customer impedes commitment. Periodically calling, messaging, or stopping by a customer's office creates a rhythm. We demonstrate caring. As much as small talk is derided, it generates familiarity. Just as we want our garden to have many types of fruits and vegetables, we also want to develop many different types of relationships from the executive suite to the individual contributor. Never underestimate the power of the individual contributor who one day could be a primary customer or assist in influencing other stakeholders. Commitment should be offered to all levels and types of customers. Moreover, there is the added benefit that individual contributors are among the most knowledgeable. Connect with customers on social media as company culture and rules allow. Social media is today's virtual community and a powerful way to build relationships.

Growing a garden is also about energy and getting plenty of sunlight. Be energetic and positive when interacting with customers in the hallway or meetings. Positivity is contagious and leaves a lasting impression. A negative or overly serious internal auditor detracts from commitment. Positivity comes through our tone of voice by being upbeat and our body language by being open and making eye contact. Closed body language, for example, having your hands in your pockets, crossing your arms, or avoiding customer interaction, can leave a bad impression. Seek out customers in common areas to make a connection. Building familiarity supports commitment.

Growing a garden requires nourishment as does developing customer relationships. Sharing valuable information such as best practices, industry articles on regulatory changes, or cross-organizational knowledge all provide nourishment. Larry Weber, global entrepreneur and public relations expert, says, "As you've noticed, people don't want to be sold. What people do want is news and information about the things they care about."[1]

Check Your Investments

Audits and projects require a significant investment of time and resources. Projects can span weeks or months. Estimate the total cost or what we'll call an "investment" in an audit. Three auditors working eight, 45 hour workweeks, at $75 an hour represents $81,000 in cost. Two customers dedicating two, 45 hour workweeks, at $75 an hour to support the audit represents $13,500 in cost. Therefore, the overall investment for the audit would be $94,500 ($81,000 + $13,500). Ask yourself—Wouldn't you occasionally check an investment account worth $100,000? Like personal investments, we want to monitor the company's investment in completed audits. Follow up after a project is complete, and ask whether recommended changes are working as intended. Inquire about collateral effects. If an unnecessary control was eliminated, did policy exceptions arise? When an operational efficiency was implemented, did business workflow continue to operate smoothly? Ask whether further changes to the original management action plans would support customer success. Auditors typically verify that management action plans have been completed but don't ask about how the action plans affected operations. Monitoring our investment demonstrates a commitment to customer success and supports meeting our investment goals. Seymour Fine, the author of *The Marketing of Ideas and Social Issues*, said, "When a customer complains, he is doing you a special favor; he is giving you another chance to serve him to his satisfaction. You will appreciate the importance of this opportunity when you consider that the customer's alternative option was to desert you for a competitor."[2]

Be Ready and Available

Building commitment means being available and ready. Audit teams should be flexible—setting aside unscheduled hours to respond to customer requests. We need to walk the walk. Theodore M. Hesburgh said, "Unless commitment is made, there are only promises and hopes…but no plans." Reserve between 10% and 30% of audit hours for customer and management requests once relationships have been established. Flexibility is particularly important in the age of business agility. Audit teams must be agile.

On very short notice, a long-standing international customer once asked my team to evaluate a significant operational change. Commitment had been established, so the customer was comfortable asking for help. As part of the special project, we discovered through data analytics that a subcontractor overbilled the company by $30 million. The customer trusted us, we responded timely, and provided a value-added service. The company recovered the funds with internal audit's assistance. The customer looked smart by bringing in a trusted advisor and discovering the discrepancy. Internal audit burnished its reputation as a committed partner.

Agility is becoming more important as velocity and volatility in the business environment increase. The much-discussed PwC 2017 State of the Internal Audit Profession Study dedicated considerable time to this point. The Study points to something most of us have observed: "Disruptions are no longer episodic; in fact, they are constant, ranging from disruptive innovation that creates a new market, to economic volatility, regulatory changes or even a catastrophic event. This fast-changing, unpredictable environment necessitates that businesses anticipate and react to all kinds of change to survive and thrive." The internal audit profession needs to disrupt itself. Being ready and available to collaborate with our customers is key in that regard.

Flex Your Muscles

No—not your biceps. Flex your mental muscles to support customers. Go above and beyond to solve a problem. Ask the question—have I done enough to help this customer? This can be in the form of large and small things.

- Can you help me better understand sales function controls?
- How do I interpret a company policy?
- Who in the organization is responsible for a particular process?
- What is the best way to work with Kevin in Supply Chain?

Bridging the divide between stakeholders and functions adds value. Who hasn't been in a situation where finding an answer to a difficult question seems impossible? We get passed from one party to the next. Internal audit knows all of the players, all of the processes. We should help answer those questions! Message your contacts and connect the dots. Internal audit has muscle, so use it for good.

Audit Liaisons

Establish audit liaisons for major areas of the business and operations. The audit liaison maintains a relationship with an individual customer or set of customers. Liaisons demonstrate ongoing commitment to understanding customer challenges and risks. This also creates a single audit point of contact for the organization.

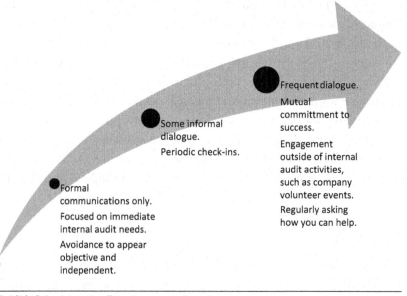

Frequent dialogue.
Mutual committment to success.
Engagement outside of internal audit activities, such as company volunteer events.
Regularly asking how you can help.

Some informal dialogue.
Periodic check-ins.

Formal communications only.
Focused on immediate internal audit needs.
Avoidance to appear objective and independent.

Exhibit 2.1   Internal audit customer commitment curve.

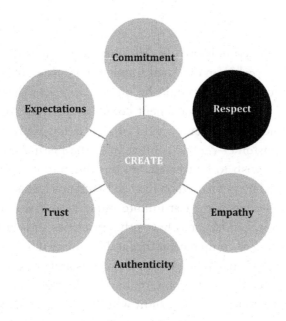

Respect

Did Mark demonstrate respect for Lindsey when he asked for documentation without sufficient notice and from a time zone with a 12 hour difference? Each of us needs to understand what respect means for our customer, and each customer may have a different perspective. Asking instead of telling is a good start. Mark lost an opportunity to ask Lindsey about her engagement preferences.

Rodney Dangerfield famously said, "I don't get no respect." The same holds true for many audit customers. They've held their roles for years. Along comes the well-intentioned internal auditor. The auditor offers advice, undervaluing the customer's experience. Internal auditors have a reputation for prescribing solutions, despite a lack of deep knowledge about the subject matter, and can seem authoritarian. Every auditee has experienced this at one time. Appreciate and respect the significant experience of customers. Be mindful of internal audit's limitations. We must center our perspective on the needs of customers and not ourselves.

Customer Centric

The oft-mentioned golden rule, "do unto others as you would have them do unto *you*" is an outdated frame of reference. The focus is on *our* preferences when it should be on the *customer*. The customer's preferred approach to engagement could be different for a host of reasons including experience, regional association, culture, and age. Embrace a customer-centric context with the platinum rule, "treat others as *they* wish to be treated." In our illustration at the start of the chapter, Mark is focused on his needs and not Lindsey's. He may be comfortable receiving last-minute requests and working late at night; however, Lindsey may have other priorities and can't respond. Mark is rushing to complete another audit—focused on his efficiency metric. Lindsey is balancing multiple projects and doesn't care about an arbitrary deadline set by internal audit. Mark needs to ask and not tell the customer how the audit will be managed. By asking, we frame the audit on the customer's terms. How would the customer like us to partner? What is the most effective means of communication? What would the customer like to get from the audit? What does a successful audit look like? What sensitivities should the audit team have about working at this location? Author Shari L. Dew wrote, "True leaders understand that leadership is not about them but about those they serve. It is not about exalting themselves but about lifting others up."

Listening Tour

Every Chief Audit Executive (CAE) should spend time listening and gaining knowledge about a customer's business before opining on a solution. We need to earn our customer's respect and that takes time. Former Imation CEO Mark Lucas spent a year as Chief Operating Officer (COO) gathering information, learning about the business and its people, and validating his assumptions to make sure he wasn't solving the wrong problem.[3] Likewise, internal auditors should take the time to understand customer operations, challenges, and priorities. This measured approach builds respect.

Acknowledgment

By acknowledging our customer's experience, we build respect and communicate our intention to collaborate. Research the customer's background by speaking with colleagues, and obtaining relevant company information. Ask about their prior experiences and how it's shaped current views of the job. Acknowledgment builds respect and eases potential conflict. A non-respectful auditor may come blazing into an audit, touting their knowledge in an effort to impress or bully the customer. The customer is unlikely to react positively. Auditors rarely have deep knowledge in more than a few disciplines. We partner with customers to identify potential issues. An expert in their field could easily misdirect an auditor if respect has not been established. Author Margaret J. Wheatley wrote, "Our willingness to acknowledge that we only see half the picture creates the conditions that make us more attractive to others. The more sincerely we acknowledge our need for their different insights and perspectives, the more they will be magnetized to join us."

Know Your Customer

It's critical to know and understand your customer. Do some sleuthing. Talk to those that understand them best. Who's worked with them in the past? I've worked for four CFOs and three Audit Committee (AC) Chairs over the past 7 years. You can bet each is unique with varying expectations. Look to a broader network—who has worked with them at other companies? What are their pet peeves? Develop a list of promoted and avoidant behaviors for key relationships (CEO, CFO, AC Chair, etc.). Break down these do's and don'ts into categories such as verbal communication, written communication, meeting protocols, work product/deliverables, and general expectations.

I Do Declare!

Statements, especially by auditors, can build defensive postures instead of collaboration and mutual respect. Customers pay close attention to what we say and how we say it. Making statements can trigger an emotional response according to Laura Wilcox, director

Exhibit 2.2 Know Your Customer

FICTIONAL EXAMPLE—KNOW YOUR CUSTOMER		
STAKEHOLDER: CEO		
CATEGORY	PROMOTE	AVOID
Verbal communications	• Provide clear and concise answers • Be conversational	• Equivocation • Excess formality
Written communications	• Copy all relevant parties on communications • Focus on data and process • Start with personal greeting • Provide solution options	• Appreciate what is appropriate for a written communication vs. a verbal discussion • Use the words XX, XX, XX
Meeting protocols	• Clear all materials in advance via walk-through meeting • Sit adjacent to answer questions • No surprises	• Answer questions when data is lacking or incomplete
General expectations	• Personal accountability	• Handshaking

of Harvard Professional Development. "With the slightest provocation, our ability to apply reason and logic can drop by 75 percent," she says. "Using questions instead of statements can also help avoid triggering emotional hijacks in others. Our feeling mind wants to sense that we are included, autonomous, competent, valued, respected, and safe."[4]

Imagine an opening meeting where an auditor says there are issues with a process. A barrier goes up and a fight instinct sets in immediately. The tone has been set. The customer views the auditor as biased, fears for their job, and may work to undermine the effort. Instead, we could ask what areas would be helpful to evaluate. The customer is now positively engaged by providing input on the objectives and scope of the review, and buying into the direction of the audit. They're invested. Emotional barriers are down allowing cognitive skills to engage.

Customers will seek collaboration when a constructive relationship has been formed. Avoid using pre-judgmental statements throughout the audit. When possible, shift toward questions.

Opening Meeting—Contrasting Examples

As a Statement:
- We will identify controls weaknesses.

As a Question:
- How can we best add value?
- Are there areas on which we should focus?
- What is your vision of the ideal process?

In the above example, the statement has a negative implication and frames the interaction for conflict. The auditor is stating that they will do something that will have a negative outcome. There is a presumption of fault. Affirmation is absent. Using questions—the context is positive. The focus is on benefit to the customer. The questions are open and create possibilities. Respect is established. Critics may say this approach precludes us from assessing high-risk areas or infringes on our independence—it doesn't. It simply offers customers the opportunity to participate in a collaborative manner.

Culture Counts

Cultural norms vary widely around the world. In Japan, the presentation of a traditional business card is important, and the card is studied before setting it aside. In the Middle East, caution is taken not to show the bottom of one's shoe. In France, business discussions may feel like debate, and patience is important. In Spain, there may be an expectation of conducting business during dinner or later in the evening. The bottom line—the auditor needs to appreciate the customer's culture. The same is true regarding company subcultures. The culture in Dallas may be quite different from the culture in San Francisco. Likewise, cultural norms vary across industries and within businesses.

There are cultures influenced by the military. Large government contractors provide products and services to senior military customers, who have specific ways of operating. Those behaviors become embedded in management operations. Formality is important, and traditional chain of command decision-making is customary. Working with a customer in this environment and building respect require understanding the chain of command and being certain to include all relevant parties. The technology industry offers a stark contrast.

Established, large technology companies tend to have more conventional decision-making cultures, whereas start-ups have egalitarian tendencies. At many start-ups, the junior, newly hired engineer may have as much sway as an experienced architect, or a founder. Likewise, within other industries, the culture may be egalitarian, while encouraging decision-making by committee.

Academic-influenced institutions, from colleges and universities to not-for-profits, support individual voices as part of a larger decision-making model. Everyone's voice is heard, and then solutions are evaluated by a cross-representation of stakeholders. Here again, the individual researcher may carry as much influence as a high-level manager. All of this highlights the varied behaviors of different institutions and that respect is heavily influenced by culture. Human resource (HR) departments can be a valuable partner in gaining appreciation for cultural norms. HR personnel have a deep understanding of organizational behavior and can provide insights into individual personality preferences. Doing a little research can reap large dividends.

The Significance and Insignificance of Titles

Have you ever met people who rely on his, her, or their title for a sense of importance? How did it make you feel? Titles play useful roles in traditional organizations to maintain order and control but have less significance in younger companies and industries. Similarly, generational differences affect the perceived importance of titles. Generally, appreciating customers for who they are and what they offer regarding knowledge and contributions demonstrates respect. Some of the most knowledgeable people are individual contributors who make things happen. We still need to recognize people based on title, educational accomplishments (PhD), or other status (Admiral) when it's suitable to the culture. The use of titles goes back to the Platinum Rule—treat each person as they wish to be treated. On the flip side, internal auditors should be careful when relying on their title. The customer doesn't care if we're a director, a manager, or a senior, they simply see an internal auditor until we earn their respect. A famous Malayan proverb says, "One can pay back the loan of gold, but one dies forever in debt to those who are kind."

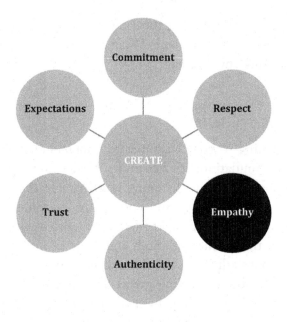

Empathy

Empathy is the ability to understand and share the feelings of other people. As internal auditors, we often focus on the task at hand and ignore the human element of working with a diverse group of individuals with varying life and work experiences. Being empathetic is not innate to everyone. However, there is a way to better understand and appreciate a customer's experience, by walking in their shoes.

Walk in Their Shoes

Walking in your customer's shoes is done by joining them on the job for a day, a week, a month, etc. It's an opportunity to appreciate more deeply and empathize with the challenges of their circumstances. Doing this provides many benefits: greater understanding of customer processes; awareness of decision-making, politics, and influence within the customer's function; and cognizance of how things operate including internal controls. The customer benefits too—they appreciate that internal audit is genuinely interested in supporting their success and may be more likely to reach out to internal audit for advice when challenges arise.

Ask questions. What about their job is challenging? What obstacles do they regularly encounter? What role do technology and data play in their work environment?

Active Listening and Observation

Start by listening to your customer to understand. In this hectic age of over stimulation, it's becoming harder and harder to just listen to someone. Active listening is a valuable skill. Physically position your body to face and engage the customer. Ask them about their work challenges. At first, simply listen without adding too much to the discussion. Body language is important. Make eye contact that's affirming. Looking directly into your customer's eyes, indicates you are paying attention. Maintain body posture that is open and welcoming by avoiding crossed arms. Keeping your arms outstretched at a table, for instance, sends a welcoming signal. Understand what the customer is really telling you. *Psychology Today* notes that 7% of communication is through the words used, 38% is through tone, and a whopping 55% is through body language.[5]

As part of active listening, avoid being judgmental. Everyone has experienced the well-intentioned friend or family member, who, upon hearing about a problem, quickly launches into what you did wrong or proposing solutions. Offering solutions is human nature. We want to resolve the issue at hand and feel rewarded by helping someone. But offering solutions can quickly shut down the conversation and negatively impact the interaction.

Affirmation

Gently affirming what they are saying solidifies empathy. Simply saying "I hear you" goes a long way. In the rush of business, we rarely take the time to provide positive feedback in our discussions. Other affirmations may include "I understand," "Tell me more," and "That's interesting." Complete agreement isn't necessary, just the act of affirming builds empathy.

Ask

When the time feels right, ask follow-up, open-ended questions. Asking non-judgmental (non-leading) questions demonstrates genuine interest in the conversation. This may seem obvious, but as auditors, we can be too focused on efficiency and not following where the conversations may lead us. Think of conversations as interesting possibilities. Open-ended questions can produce important discoveries that bring greater meaning to the relationship and understanding the person. Listen to the responses with determination. Circle back to the active listening techniques used earlier.

Filters

All of us at one time, some more than others, unwittingly apply filters to the information we receive. Life experiences shape our perceptions. It's hard not to apply preconceived notions. We carry biases at some level based on our upbringing, environment, and experiences. Acknowledging those preconceptions and biases is important to ensure we are fully present, that is to say invested, in the conversation. Understanding how filters affect other people impacts how successfully we will be engaging with customers and demonstrating empathy. Be mindful about filters related to age, education, gender, race, sexual orientation and gender identity, religion, culture, differing abilities, life experiences, and economic situation. Seek greater understanding about the whole person to successfully empathize.

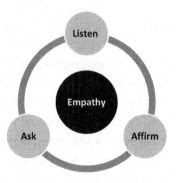

Exhibit 2.3 Building empathy.

Authenticity

Authenticity is being true to one's own personality, spirit, or character. Attempting to alter behavior to mirror someone is sometimes suggested as a way to seem relatable. If done poorly, it can seem manipulative and inauthentic. Understanding your own personality lends to more authenticity.

Self-Awareness

Self-awareness helps us understand our impact on other people. Psychologist Tasha Eurich, author of the book *Insight*, says that on a good day, "80 percent of us are lying to ourselves about whether we're lying to ourselves." Self-awareness is made up of two parts—internal self-awareness and external self-awareness. Internal self-awareness is the ability to introspect and recognize your authentic self. External self-awareness is the ability to recognize how you fit in with the rest of the world.[6] Going through a self-awareness awakening leads to authenticity, yet can be a painful process, especially when soliciting feedback from others through 360 reviews and emotional intelligence evaluations. Audit customers are sensitive to whether we are being authentic, which also broadcasts truthfulness and trustworthiness.

Excess introspection can be unhealthy when it bleeds into interactions. Think of the insecure auditor that projects puffery and unjustified confidence or on the opposite end of the spectrum, meekness and a lack of self-assurance. Not knowing yourself brings out bad behaviors.

The second element, Dr. Eurich points out, is external self-awareness. Understanding how we fit into our organizational culture and leveraging that information successfully impact how much value we can provide. Auditors working in a collaborative environment that unknowingly have a policing attitude limit their contributions and hinder customer relationship development. Each organization's culture is different. Understanding those differences and how to fit in is critical.

Earnest Interaction

Avoid telling customers what you think they want to hear. Engage in mutually respectful, yet honest discussions. Authenticity demands honesty. Honesty does not, however, require being discourteous. It's a delicate balance.

Life Experiences

Draw on life experiences to be more relatable and authentic. Sharing personal experiences builds bonds. Safely sharing vulnerabilities can be powerful as well. Discussing something you've learned about yourself and how it informs your approach to relationship management can spur greater closeness and humanize the internal audit role. Once when I was doing audit work in Spain, I inquired about Hotline reports or investigations. My Spanish counterpart chuckled. I thought it was a strange reaction, and then he explained that a Hotline in Spain is a dating line, not a reference to an ethics reporting line. Funny anecdotes like this can ease tensions. A May 2014, *Harvard Business Review* article by Jeanine Prime and Elizabeth Salib recommended sharing mistakes as teachable moments. "When leaders showcase their own personal growth, they legitimize the growth and learning of others; by admitting to their own imperfections, they make it okay for others to be fallible, too."[7]

Recalling difficult life experiences builds strength to help us overcome new trials and tribulations. Although a current work problem may seem stressful, there are undoubtedly past experiences that we've worked through successfully that were more difficult. Keeping those experiences with us and using them in a healthy manner make our interactions more real and authentic for customers. One of the most authentic people I've known was my mother, Sylvia. She was raised on a farm in Vermont by her grandparents with the help of many aunts and uncles. Sylvia's mother died within months of her birth. Her father worked multiple jobs and was a good person but didn't have the time nor resources to raise her. She graduated from high school and went on to become a registered nurse, where her genuine authenticity and empathy helped countless seniors during their sunset years. Not much phased my mother because she used her life experiences to relate to the customer, the residents at the nursing home, where she worked. Keep one or two of those difficult circumstances with you for strength and use them to be true to yourself and your customer.

Be Present

Authenticity requires being fully present with the customer. There are numerous distractions vying for our attention. Set aside mobile devices and clear your mind of other thoughts to focus on the present interaction. It's hard enough to be authentic when you're 100% committed to the discussion, let alone, when you're thinking about the next meeting, the status of a project, or what you're having for dinner. People appreciate being truly heard.

Realistic Commitments

Authenticity demands being realistic about the commitments we make. Committing to unrealistic expectations with the customer that later prove to be undeliverable diminishes our credibility. The old adage to under promise and over deliver remains relevant. A pattern of failing to fulfill promises degrades our ability to work with a customer and ask for help when in need.

Humility

Being authentic works best with humility. Humility is placing the needs of others ahead of yourself. We should disregard our status as a manager, a director, or a vice president and focus on the quality and intent of the interaction. Role titles and perceived powers separate us from the customer. It's far more meaningful to find common cause and understanding than to use coercive tactics to influence. Some of the greatest leaders in the world have showed levels of humility: Mahatma Gandhi, George Washington, Mother Theresa, Benjamin Franklin, Warren Buffet, Pope Francis, and Angela Merkel. Internal auditors should be judicious in referencing internal audit charters, reporting lines to the board of directors and executive management, and other means of establishing authority. The development of personal relationships will provide more bountiful results for all involved. When assessing authenticity, consider the following behaviors.

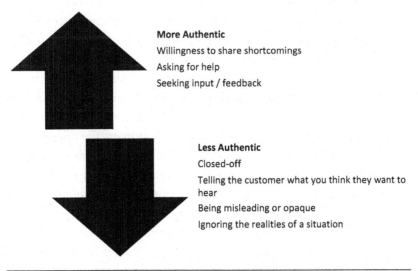

More Authentic
Willingness to share shortcomings
Asking for help
Seeking input / feedback

Less Authentic
Closed-off
Telling the customer what you think they want to hear
Being misleading or opaque
Ignoring the realities of a situation

Exhibit 2.4 Building authenticity.

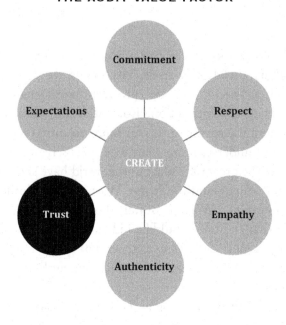

Trust

Trust is the foundation of successful, long-term relationships. The same holds true for internal auditors and their customers. Internal auditors are challenged by competing demands as an advisor, a confidante, and a protector of shareholder interests on behalf of the board of directors. The more seasoned auditor understands that not all issues require raising the alarm bell to management or the Audit Committee. Many matters can be resolved through collaboration and problem-solving. So long as it's not a matter of ethics or fraud, many issues can be handled at the process owner level by partnering to improve controls around a process. When it is necessary to raise an issue to the executive team or Audit Committee for non-fraud-related matters, it's critical to afford customers the opportunity to fully understand the issue first. Before any audit observation is finalized, we should always explore mitigating control practices. If not, we are failing to provide fair treatment and proper context. This means providing an opportunity to explore compensating controls. Here we play an important role as process and risk experts. We facilitate the discussion. Customers are focused on achieving their goals and may not recognize that other practices are controls. Leading this dialog builds trust by demonstrating an investment in their success and adds value by helping them better understand their processes. It can also lead to optimizing the control structure. Perhaps the informal compensating control is more meaningful than the official control, and duplicative controls can be eliminated.

Achieving trust happens when we've demonstrated a pattern of helping our customer achieve their objectives. As Richard Chambers, the CEO of the IIA, says in his book *Trusted Advisors*, "We can't just show up, articulate our views about risks, and expect people to heed our advice without first earning their trust. Neither can we expect them to respond favorably to our assurance work." So how do we do that? We need to engage early and often and find opportunities outside of formal audits to provide value.

Knowledge Sharing

One simple way to build trust is to consistently share meaningful information. Research regulatory developments, emerging practices, and current events that potentially impact your customer. Send a simple email saying, "I came across this article and thought it may be of interest." The context should be nondirective. There are many white papers and benchmarking studies on various topics written throughout the year. Monitoring the issuance and sharing the results of these studies add value to our customer and build trust. Each year, Grant Thornton publishes a study on Government Contracting practices based on an extensive survey of companies. I shared the results with the business development and finance leadership team. The study helped develop a better-informed strategy. Technology has enabled the easy monitoring of information. Set up a Google alert on a given topic, and developments in that area are sent to your inbox daily. Type in a key word or phrase and Google will send a daily summary of any Internet articles or mentions related to the topic chosen. Sharing relevant articles about proposed or emerging changes to regulatory requirements demonstrates trust building by helping our customers to plan for the needed changes to their practices. The best part is, once trust has been established, the customer may reach back to internal audit and request help in evaluating their current processes to plan for the redesign to account for the new regulatory requirement. Lastly, once the new process is in place, both the customer and internal audit have more confidence that risk will be mitigated. It creates win–win solutions. Internal audit has added value at the front end by proactively sharing information, consulting on process redesign, and providing assurance that risk has been managed.

Sources of information to share include:

- Professional journals related to human resources, supply chain, information technology, finance, and engineering
- Industry publications (manufacturing, financial services, technology, government, health care, marketing, etc.)
- Trade publications
- University journals and resources
- Subscription services and subscriber databases, such as Gartner
- Magazines, such as *CFO* or *Inc.*
- Meet-up events
- Original research via employee surveys or data analysis

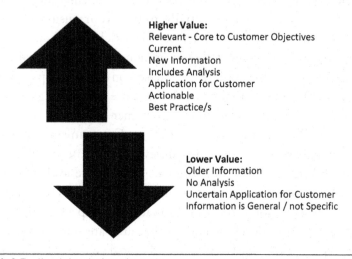

Higher Value:
Relevant - Core to Customer Objectives
Current
New Information
Includes Analysis
Application for Customer
Actionable
Best Practice/s

Lower Value:
Older Information
No Analysis
Uncertain Application for Customer
Information is General / not Specific

Exhibit 2.5   Knowledge sharing value scale.

Transparency

Imagine a friend coming to visit and staying at your house for a vacation. Everyone is enjoying themselves catching up on old times. You stock the refrigerator with extra groceries, forgo your normal routine, and make every effort to accommodate your guests. As the week concludes, and your guest is scheduled to depart, they drop a bombshell—they've lost their job and have no place to live. Of course, you want to help. But why wasn't the friend transparent about the situation from the beginning? Has trust been broken? Now imagine a situation at work with a customer. Internal audit visits a regional office to meet with the site manager to better understand operations. Without warning, the auditor reports perceived issues to the executive team back at headquarters. The customer is caught off-guard and feels deceived about the intent of the visit. Trust is broken. It's important to be forthright with customers whenever possible. A lack of transparency creates suspicion and destroys credibility. Likewise, never give the impression that "everything is fine," and then surprise the customer at the closing meeting with a new observation or potential issue. Those surprises are unwanted guests at the closing meeting that create long-term, if not permanent, trust issues. I offer a "no surprises guarantee" and flow that expectation down to all team members. That's not to say you won't discover potential concerns toward the end of an engagement. However, the new information needs to be communicated quickly and appropriately to allow all applicable stakeholders sufficient time to research, validate, and respond to the concern.

Celebrate Success!

A basic human need is to feel appreciated. So, we should celebrate the good every day and whenever possible. Highlighting positive achievements is a radical way to change customer perceptions about internal audit. Use success stories to reinforce behavior. One of internal audit's roles is to monitor and report on the effectiveness of controls. Reporting frequently focuses on exceptions and overlooks highlighting controls that are working. For example, at SRI, I email the head of each business division, along with the CEO and president, the names of employees who had 100% compliance in completing daily timekeeping records for the year. Accurate and timely recording of hours is critical in our business due to regulatory requirements. Timekeeping can be a drag. For those employees that demonstrate unparalleled commitment, I make a point to celebrate their success. This builds trust with the individual employee and the corresponding executive. Highlighting positive information demonstrates that internal audit is there to help employees succeed.

Celebrating success demonstrates a deeper understanding of customer activities. When customers improve a process by making it more efficient, touting that achievement shows that we have taken the time to understand their business and builds trust for internal audit to evaluate other processes in the future. Give credit instead of taking credit. Over the years, I've partnered with various process owners to identify cost-saving opportunities within their span of control. We made a concerted effort to give credit to the customer for any savings identified, understanding that this developed trust with the customer. All that matters are that the customer and company benefited from the collaboration.

Catch people doing good things by making a concerted effort to identify the positive. Audit Committees hear a lot about risks but less about what's working well. Internal auditors should recognize customers who are making positive changes and improving controls. Nelson Mandela said, "It is better to put others in front, especially when you celebrate victory when nice things occur. You take the front line when there is danger. Then people will appreciate your leadership."

Confidentiality

When trust has been established, people are willing to share concerns or observations more freely with some expectation that it will remain confidential. Internal auditors must use good judgment as to when a concern should be acted upon. Fraud, theft, and workplace harassment or abuse are among the things that must be investigated or elevated to management for further action. In those cases, we must be careful to protect the person reporting the concern from retribution by not disclosing their identity if possible. The ethics officer is a great partner in these situations.

Aside from serious concerns, we all have had a customer complain about a colleague's personal style, approach to management, or solution to a problem. It's important for us to listen and avoid judging. The information provided can shape a greater understanding of business operations and challenges and when appropriate should remain confidential. It's important not to gossip or spread subjective information. Avoid office politics and the perception that you're a source of watercooler information. This is a quick way to lose customer trust.

We also need to be aware that some individuals may share information to try to manipulate a situation. Maintaining integrity is critical.

Be Human

Being human. It might sound a bit strange and obvious. Yet, we sometimes forget to bring a human element to our business relationships.
Internal auditors, in particular, are hesitant to acknowledge vulnerability with customers for fear that it may undermine their credibility.
How can we expect our customers to open up to us, if we are unwill-
ing to do the same with them? There are few things that ease tensions
faster than self-deprecating humor when done appropriately. Likewise,
sharing vulnerabilities in a modest manner can be powerful in building
trusting relationships. This doesn't mean sharing your deepest secrets.
It's about demonstrating that we all share a common, human experience and are fallible. Why is that important? Because average audit
customers have a preconceived notion that they are being judged. If we
can break that filter, we begin to build trusting and lasting relationships, which are non-transactional. Internal audit already brings built-
in authority to its relationships through its reporting structure in the
organization, its reporting line to the board of directors, and the internal audit charter, which commands independence and access to people
and resources. So, further emphasizing authority over more relatable
vulnerability is not helpful. Emphasize being human and mutually
vulnerable. That's not to say we should share all of our weaknesses, but
it does mean being open about our common human fallibility. Emma
Seppala, the associate director of Stanford University's Center for
Compassion and Altruism Research and Education, states, "As leaders
and employees, we are often taught to keep a distance and project a certain image. An image of confidence, competence, and authority. We
may disclose our vulnerability to a spouse or close friend behind closed
doors at night but we would never show it elsewhere during the day, let
alone at work." She goes on to say that "once you show your vulnerabilities in an authentic way, a bond results that can pay off later."[8] Another
way to show vulnerability is to simply ask for help. This is particularly
powerful coming from an auditor because it implies that we need our
customer's support. Harry Gordon Selfridge said, "Goodwill is the one
and only asset that competition cannot undersell or destroy."

Exhibit 2.6 Trust ladder. Use the trust ladder to build confidence.

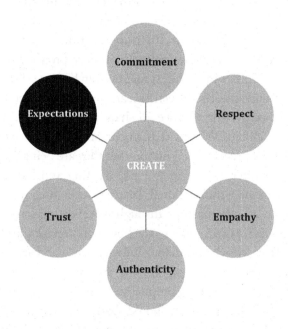

Expectations

Now that we've set a foundation to create mutually beneficial and healthy customer relationships, we need to ensure we understand expectations. Roy H. Williams, author of *Wizard of Ads*, says, "The first step in exceeding your customer's expectations is to know those expectations." Ask questions. Ask about the customer's personal goals and objectives. Ask about their preferred methods of communication. Ask about what is valuable. Allison Wood Brooks and Leslie K. John write in the *Harvard Business Review* that most people don't grasp that asking a lot of questions unlocks learning and improves interpersonal bonding. They go on to say that follow-up questions, in particular, signal to partners that we are listening, care, and want to know more. "People interacting with a conversation partner who asks lots of follow-up questions tend to feel respected and heard."[9]

Goals, Strategy, Objectives, and Tactics

It's hard to effectively meet expectations if we don't understand our customer's goals, strategy, objectives, and tactics. Mikal E. Belicove, a contributor for *Forbes Magazine*, defines a goal as "a broad primary outcome," a strategy as "the approach you take to achieve a goal," an objective as "a measurable step you take to achieve a strategy," and a tactic as "a tool you use in pursuing an objective associated with a strategy."[10] The answers to each of these points will help us better understand expectations. A business president focused on the company becoming one of the three largest providers in the industry may have different expectations than a COO with a goal to make the company financially sustainable over the next 12 months. Ensure discussions are forward looking, so internal audit can anticipate how to add value over mid- to long-term time frames. Understand customer expectations related to goals, strategy, objectives, and tactics for opportunities to add value as the risk expert in the organization, through audits and special projects, or as a consultant. Asking about goals, strategy, objectives, and tactics can be educational for both the customer and internal audit. The executive team may be able to clearly articulate each. Can the same be said at the functional owner level? Have the HR, finance, information technology, marketing, or supply chain organizations clearly defined their goals, strategy, objectives, and tactics? Is each function aligned with the overall enterprise vision? Asking these questions adds value and helps customers assess alignment with enterprise efforts. The information gathered also supports the development of effective value propositions, discussed in a separate chapter.

Use the following Goal, Strategy, Objectives, and Tactic Expectations Matrix to facilitate this process:

Exhibit 2.7   Goal, Strategy, Objectives, and Tactic Expectations Matrix Template

	DESCRIPTION	EXPECTATION/S LIST CUSTOMER EXPECTATIONS OF INTERNAL AUDIT FOR EACH CATEGORY
Goal	A broad primary outcome	
Strategy	The approach you take to achieve a goal	
Objectives	A measurable step you take to achieve a strategy	
Tactic	A tool used in pursuing an objective	

Exhibit 2.8   Goal, Strategy, Objectives, Tactic, President Example

	DESCRIPTION	EXPECTATION/S
Goal	Become one of the three largest providers of distributed manufacturing equipment.	Research industry benchmarking information on revenue-to-staffing ratios.
Strategy	Grow the business by 20% over the next 36 months.	Facilitate a risk assessment of current company processes and systems to determine readiness in supporting the strategy and identify potential gaps. Make operational recommendations to support the strategy.
Objectives	Identify customer needs not directly addressed by the company.	Identify regulatory requirements, market risk, and other relevant information related to areas currently not addressed by the company.
Tactic	Acquire or merge with two of the top five companies in the vertical chain.	Support the due diligence process during acquisitions. Provide management with risk profiles for acquisition targets.

Exhibit 2.9   Goal, Strategy, Objectives, Tactic, COO Example

	DESCRIPTION	EXPECTATION/S LIST CUSTOMER EXPECTATIONS OF INTERNAL AUDIT FOR EACH CATEGORY
Goal	Position the company to be financially self-sustaining.	Evaluate management reporting and data available to support the goal.
Strategy	Improve profitability by 5%.	Identify product lines that are not profitable and perform root cause analyses.
Objectives	Reduce operating costs by 10%.	Evaluate processes for automation opportunities.
Tactic	Identify process inefficiencies.	Identify duplicative controls for elimination or ways to optimize controls performance.

Aligning internal audit work to company and customer goals, strategy, objectives, and tactics increases value and steers efforts to forward-looking risks and potential control issues. We should always be able to answer the question—how does internal audit's work relate to the company's strategic plan?

Communication

There are entire books dedicated to communication theory. For the purposes of this book, we're interested in understanding customer communication expectations. Different customers will have different expectations. Ask customers what they value in terms of communication, when they want to hear from us, and how they want us to communicate with them. We have a broad set of customers: the AC, the executive team, internal process owners, employees of the company, and external parties, such as regulators. Each one will have different expectations around communications.

Audit Committee Communications

A key customer is the AC Chair and AC members. We have a responsibility to provide them with valuable insights to help them provide oversight. An article in *Business Insider* suggests providing board members with clear and concise information regarding issues facing management and the company. "Being clear and concise ensures that they have the quality information they need to make quick and accurate decisions. Don't overwhelm them with data and get them in the weeds."[11]

In preparation for this book, we surveyed over 100 CAEs through the IIA's Audit Executive Center and asked their perspective on AC member communication expectations. All communications must consider individual preferences, organizational culture, and historical practices. The following summarizes key themes from the CAEs surveyed.

Valuable to hear

- New and useful insights. AC Chairs will be interested in your perspective and concerns vs. executive management.
- A heads-up about potential controversial topics prior to the AC meeting.

- Connecting the dots between the results of audit work and board priorities.
- Benchmarking information vs. other organizations.
- A summary of the quarterly report prior to scheduled AC meetings.
- Information on risks before realization. Add deep dives of risk discussion topics to quarterly agendas.
- Connection between AC discussions and other board of director committee topics of interest.
- Current topics being discussed by outside boards.
- Insights into the tone at the top.
- Anything additional that helps AC menbers fulfill their obligations as it relates to internal audit.
- What's working in enterprise and within the internal audit organization.

When to communicate

- Meet before Committee meetings to discuss topics to be discussed with the full Committee.
- Meet after Committee meetings to identify unstated follow-up items. Depending on the personality, the Chair may share open questions for follow-up items from executive sessions.
- Use off-cycle meetings with the Chair to discuss longer term Committee needs, for example, the AC Charter and Committee information/training needs.
- Understand and promptly respond to Committee questions and requests.
- Avoid bringing items to the Chair that have not been discussed with the executive team, unless it is related to fraud involving management.
- Insist on having an executive session at every AC meeting. Use that time to explain the differences of opinion with management and how you plan to resolve them. Make sure these are major items worth discussing and that they have been previously discussed with the administrative reporting line and the AC Chair.

How to communicate

- Use AC Chair time productively—focus on the quality of conversations. Keep your key messages short, sweet, and to the point.
- Engage in consistent, well-established, and permanent communication.
- Use clear and concise messaging. Unclear or subjective communications can lead to surprises.
- Be mindful about consistency in messages between the AC and management team. What have been prior messages about specific topics? Have you properly prepared the AC Chair and AC members for the message being delivered?
- Avoid unintentional conflicting messages with management or external audit partners.
- Be the truth teller. Always answer director questions factually with information gathered firsthand. Never pass on hearsay.
- Assume the Committee has read all materials and use Committee time for value-added discussions.
- Keep in mind that the AC has "oversight" responsibilities—don't pull them or let them drift into management.
- Find the right reporting format based on AC Chair and member preferences.
- Avoid burdening AC Chair with unnecessary details.
- Always take the extra steps to make information easily digestible. Provide highlights.

The Executive Team

One of the biggest relationship challenges is balancing the needs of our executive team members with AC expectations. The executive team may have different priorities and therefore different expectations. This is true for communication too. Expectations are always organization and culture dependent. Our survey of CAEs indicated the following themes when communicating with the executive team:

Valuable to hear

- Emerging risks and potential solutions and options for resolving.

- Observations on the tone at the middle. Are middle managers on board with the company's strategic direction, goals, objectives, etc.? If not, what is the feedback?
- Cost-saving opportunities.
- Meaningful and relevant external benchmarking and industry data and a translation as to how it applies to the organization. Take the additional step to compare to company data.
- Keeping them informed about what's on the horizon and items that may impact strategy.
- Insights into the big picture of the enterprise.
- Information on what is being communicated to the AC Chair.

When to communicate

- Use their time wisely. They are short on time and overloaded with information.
- Communicate regularly and directly discuss expectations. Note that this does not contradict using their time wisely.
- Involve the CFO/CEO/XXX before and after AC meetings. Discuss the expectations of the meeting.
- Provide a weekly or monthly report to the CFO/CEO/XXX on your organization's plan/project/audit status.

How to communicate

- Make sure you are fair. Stick to the facts. Be kind in the manner in which you present issues.
- Don't create political drama. Handle peer conflicts.
- Put reports in context. Give credit for positive things.
- Know that the executive team will talk to the AC Chair, so keep your story consistent when you have something to share.
- Avoid surprises.
- Be as open and trusting in communications as possible. Leadership is generally concerned that you are "telling" the AC something thay they aren't aware of. Be transparent and open in both relationships.
- Help both the executive team and the AC to see the other's point of view and foster collaboration and dialog.

- Balance the bottom-line perspective of the CFO/CEO/XXX against the perhaps more conservative risk adverse perspective of the AC Chair. Building good relationships with both parties enables the CAE to be the mediator and to help find compromise when views differ.
- Take care in what you say, opinion wise, between the administrative reporting line and the AC Chair. Make sure you have provided fair warning and opportunity to discuss.

Process Owners/Individual Contributors/Employees

Much of our day-to-day time is spent with process owner customers. These are the folks that get stuff done and help us fulfill our responsibilities. They have varying communication expectations, and we need to understand those expectations. One overriding consideration is our responsiveness to their requests. We all live in an age of advanced technology and expect on-demand services. Promptly reply to process owner inquiries. With mobile devices, we can do this virtually from anywhere, at any time. Research by Tim Pickard on changing customer expectations noted that technology is changing expectations about what we should know. Given the advent of Google, customers expect us to have answers readily available.[12]

Consider every communication with a process owner or individual contributor as an opportunity to provide them with a solution. I've fielded numerous calls over the years from process owners looking for help to identifying the right resource to resolve an issue. Use those communication opportunities to facilitate a solution. Don't pass the buck to someone else. Connect the process owner with the right resources and facilitate a dialogue to address their concern. Proactively follow-up with all parties involved to verify the customer's issue was addressed. Internal audit truly has an eagle's eye view of the enterprise and should leverage that insight and perspective in communications. The following are examples of questions I've fielded over the years:

- How should I interpret policy X for the work I'm trying to accomplish?
- Can you help me access X data in X system?
- X system is not working. Can you help me?

- I have a concern about X. What should I do?
- A change in process X is preventing me from meeting my goals. Can you help?
- Process X is very inefficient and I've tried raising it as an issue without any success. What should I do?
- You have a good relationship with person X. Can you provide pointers on how to partner with them?
- I'm concerned about an ethics issue. What should I do?

In each of these cases, the customer wasn't exactly sure who could help resolve their problem. Using these communication opportunities to go the extra mile and facilitate solutions adds value. Our process owners expect that we have answers, and if we don't, we should help them find the answer.

Deliverables/Reporting

Seek customer expectations about deliverables including style and format. Consider whether alternative forms of reporting are appropriate and possible. A PowerPoint presentation may be more meaningful than a word document or PDF. Follow the "less is more" rule and make sure to only include what's most important.

When drafting deliverables, consider the following:

- Has the report or briefing set the right tone for this particular customer? Tone is influenced by the adjectives we use. Avoid injecting emotion.
- Are the results put in context? We do a disservice when results are intentionally or unintentionally dramatized by selectively highlighting the downside and the negative. For example, stating that five of ten items tested had exceptions sounds pretty terrible. But if those five items were selected based on a high-risk pool from data analytics, it paints a different picture. We need to provide a complete picture for readers with full context to prevent improper conclusions.
- Have I provided data to support results? If data have been included, is it valuable? Does it provide deeper insight and understanding? Does the data help the reader draw the right conclusion? Could the data mislead the reader in any way?

Have the data been properly time bound—indicating what time period was covered? Have data limitations been disclosed?

- Have all relevant stakeholders been consulted? Consider how the report will be interpreted by different audiences and anticipate their questions.
- Have I been fair and balanced? Would any particular reader of the report walk away with a sense of being treated unfairly? Does the report stick to the facts—the full facts—that provide a balanced view of the given circumstances?
- Have I highlighted things that are working well? Every operation, process, and situation will have positive aspects that are working effectively. Have these been included in reporting?
- Have I given credit, where credit is due? As noted above regarding things that are working well, have we acknowledged efforts management has made to improve a process to provide context for the current state of controls? Does the report recognize the positive changes that management has proactively made while the audit was in process?
- Have I considered how the report will play out with other stakeholders and audiences? For instance, if the report is read by an external third party, will they draw improper conclusions or does the report properly stand on its own and not leap to unsupportable conclusions?
- Have I connected the dots for the reader regarding larger risk questions? Where risks are noted in the report, have they been correlated with the bigger picture for the enterprise? Are the risks disclosed meteors or pebbles? Does the report clearly articulate that they are being addressed by management action plans?
- Have the observations been noted in previous reports, and if so, what will be different this time in creating change? What will internal audit do to make sure the solution is sticky and stays in place? Has the management action plan been linked to an executive champion for accountability?
- Does the report outline value provided to the customer? What value-added deliverables were provided?
- Does the report illuminate new issues or is it just stating what was already known? Have "ah-ha" realizations been provided for the reader?

- Could someone draw the wrong conclusions from the report or is it clear enough to stand on its own?
- Is the report structure consistent throughout? Have observations been structured consistently, for instance, issue, criteria, risk and mitigating controls, root cause, and action plan?
- Have the questions "what," "how," "why," and "when" been answered?
- Does the report tie to customer goals, strategy, objectives, and tactics?
- Have risks been described in monetary terms? If so, has proper context been provided? For instance, "non-compliance could result in monetary fines up to $100,000 per instance, but this has rarely occurred."
- Have the issues in the report been presented in terms of a value proposition for the customer? Do the observations clearly articulate an urgent need related to the customer's interests?
- Would the customer be willing to "pay" the result, if this was provided by an external party or consultant?

Exhibit 2.10 Report Expectations Matrix

EXPECTATION	SATISFACTORY? (Y/N)
Tone	☐
Context	☐
Data supporting results	☐
All relevant stakeholders considered	☐
Fair and balanced	☐
Credit for effective processes	☐
Suitable for multiple audiences	☐
Connects the dots on risk	☐
Repeat issues disclosed	☐
Value provided	☐
Ah-ha realizations provided	☐
Clarity for conclusions	☐
Consistent structure	☐
What, how, why, and when	☐
Link to customer goals, strategy, objectives, and tactics	☐
Monetary linkage	☐
Articulated value proposition	☐

Expectations on Report Opinions

For years I've been asking customers, "What do you think the audit opinion should be?" vs. telling them the audit opinion. It's a good test as to whether internal audit has been collaborative and transparent throughout the audit process. When an audit has been collaborative, I've found there is consensus on the overall audit opinion, the customer is responsive to the results, and the risks identified are swiftly addressed. Eventually, this led to the elimination of audit opinions. Observations and risks were clearly communicated, and the dreaded audit opinion was no longer the focal point of the review. There are plenty of audit teams and customers that spend countless hours debating audit opinions. I've known auditors that relish the moment an audit opinion is revealed. Those discussions frequently happen at the end of the audit and create a lasting impression. Who wants to be told they are inadequate? Yes, we primarily audit processes, not people—but it's difficult for a customer not to take a negative opinion personally. What really matters is whether positive change happens!

Consider what your customers expect related to the use of audit opinions—the AC, the executive team, and process owner customers. Most importantly, be open to the discussion and flexible regarding how results are expressed and whether an overall opinion is utilized. The most important impact we can have is to help our customers reduce risk and improve the chances of them meeting their objectives.

Chapter Recap

We cannot add value without strong customer relationships. Internal audit's customer portfolio is diverse—the AC, executive management, process owner customers, and external parties, such as regulators. Discerning how to effectively create valuable relationships with each can be a challenge. Using the CREATE model provides a repeatable process for achieving long-lasting and mutually beneficial relationships.

Commit to customer success. Take time to understand customer priorities. Nurture the relationship. Grow your customer garden—providing nourishment, energy, and light. Check your investments in customers—reaching out to them throughout the year and after audits are completed to check on unintended impacts. Be ready, available, and flexible—committing means being there for our customers when they need us. Go above and beyond every time to help them solve a problem.

Show *respect* for the customer. Apply the Platinum Rule—treat the customer as they wish to be treated. Go on a listening tour to understand their needs. Acknowledge their experience. Know and understand the customer. Appreciate cultural differences and adjust style accordingly. Respect and understand the significance of organizational structures, roles, and titles.

Demonstrate *empathy* in interactions. Walk in your customers' shoes—appreciate more deeply their challenges and circumstances. Use active listening skills—be present in communications and listen to understand. Be affirming and ask questions. Be aware of personal filters when receiving information.

Be *authentic* and self-aware. Engage customers earnestly. Draw on life experiences to be more relatable. Be present in interactions by setting aside distractions, such as mobile devices. Make realistic commitments. Be humble.

Develop *trust* with the customer by demonstrating a pattern of helping them achieve their objectives. Facilitate knowledge sharing—external benchmarking, articles of interest, and other value information. Be transparent—offer a no surprises guarantee. Celebrate success—highlight positive customer achievements and elevate to the executive team. Protect confidentiality whenever possible. Be human—bring the human element to the business relationship.

Understand *expectations*—goals and objectives, communication preferences, and deliverables and reporting. Ask meaningful questions. Ensure discussions are forward looking, so internal audit can anticipate how to add value over mid- to long-term time frames. Use the Expectations Matrix. Align internal audit work accordingly. Understand the unique communication preferences of each customer type—the AC, executive management, and process owners. Consider every communication as an opportunity to provide them with solutions. Use communication as an opportunity to go the extra mile and facilitate solutions. Ensure that reporting meets expectations, and use the Report Expectations Matrix to increase the value.

Notes

1 Larry Weber, Marketing to the Social Web: How Digital Customer Communities Build Your Business, Wiley, March 2019.
2 Seymour Fine, The Marketing of Ideas and Social Issues, Praeger, August 15, 1981.
3 George Bradt, Mergers and Acquisitions Are Not Strategies. They Are Tactics, *Forbes*, September 5, 2012. www.forbes.com/sites/georgebradt/2012/09/05/mergers-and-acquisitions-are-not-strategies-they-are-tactics/#604ddab05071.
4 Laura Wilcox, Director of Harvard Professional Development. www.extension.harvard.edu/professional-development/blog/emotional-intelligence-no-soft-skill.
5 Jeff Thompson, Ph.D. *Psychology Today*. www.psychologytoday.com/us/blog/beyond-words/201109/is-nonverbal-communication-numbers-game.
6 A Beginner's Guide to Self-Awareness, Kristin Wong, The Cut. www.thecut.com/2017/10/how-to-be-more-self-aware.html.
7 The Best Leaders are Humble Leaders, Jeanine Prime and Elizabeth Salib, *Harvard Business Review*, May 12, 2014. https://hbr.org/2014/05/the-best-leaders-are-humble-leaders.
8 Why Being Vulnerable Doesn't Mean You're Being Weak, Will Yakowicz, Inc., December 16, 2014. www.inc.com/will-yakowicz/why-being-vulnerable-is-a-good-idea.html.
9 The Surprising Power of Questions, Allison Wood Brooks and Leslie K. John, *Harvard Business Review*, May–June 2018.
10 Mikal E. Belicove, Understanding Goals, Strategy, Objectives and Tactics in the Age of Social, *Forbes Magazine*, September 27, 2013. www.forbes.com/sites/mikalbelicove/2013/09/27/understanding-goals-strategies-objectives-and-tactics-in-the-age-of-social/#3fb8d35f4c79.
11 Marc P. Palker, 5 Tips to Effectively Communicate with your Board of Directors, *Business Insider*, October 23, 2015. www.businessinsider.com/5-tips-to-effectively-communicate-with-your-board-of-directors-2015-10.
12 Tim Packard, 10 Trends Changing Customer Expectations, ICMI, July 20, 2015. www.icmi.com/Resources/Customer-Experience/2015/07/10-Trends-Changing-Customer-Expectations.

Bibliography

Richard Chambers, Trusted Advisors, The Institute of Internal Auditors Research Foundation.
Tasha Eurich, Insight, www.insight-book.com.
Institute of Internal Auditors, Audit Executive Center.

PwC 2017 State of the Internal Audit Profession Study, www.pwc.com/us/en/cfodirect/issues/risk-management/internal-audit-transformation-study-2017.html.

Roy H. Williams, Wizard of Ads, Bard Press (June 2, 1998).

Stephen R. Covey. The 7 Habits of Highly Effective People: Powerful Lessons in Personal Change. www.franklincovey.com.

Factor 3
Talent

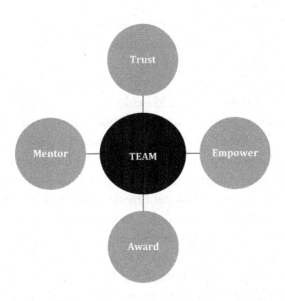

At a recent conference, I discussed the need for internal auditors to focus on value. An attendee spoke with me afterward and said he was simply trying to survive. Hopefully he was attending to learn something new and enhance his skills, but he was resistant to embrace new ideas that challenged his practices and preconceived notions. He was comfortable in his paradigm. The problem is, when we're comfortable, we should be worried. I recently shared this story with Larry Harrington, the former Vice President of Internal Audit at Raytheon. Larry, who is passionate about people development, stated the problem clearly: "We need to thrive, not survive. In a world where you just want to survive, you're letting the world dictate your professional life or death. In an environment where you thrive, you're in control." Thriving in this context is achieved through personal growth and investment, challenging yourself by raising the performance bar, taking risks, and never allowing yourself to get comfortable.

Executives responding to the World Economic Forum's 2015 Technological Tipping Points Survey said that 30% of corporate audits would be conducted by artificial intelligence by 2025. This is consistent with the Oxford Martin School study in 2010, which predicted that 47% of US jobs would be lost to automation within 10–20 years. Ignoring the realities of the future will lead to obsolescence. Embracing and proactively responding to change will position us to deliver value with greater efficiency.

In his book, *Outliers: The Story of Success*, Malcolm Gladwell discusses the 10,000-Hour Rule. Malcolm theorizes that to be an expert in any discipline, you need to gain 10,000 hours of relevant practice and experience. When we look at the speed of change today, 10,000 hours is no longer enough to support the evolution of skills needed to meet customer needs. 10,000 hours marks a fixed statistic. Our job is to always be in development mode, learning the newest technical and soft skills necessary to deliver value for customers. We must be our own talent agents, mindful of our ability to anticipate, and meet customer needs, sometimes before they know what those needs are. Therein lies the importance of the Talent Factor. Having skills to meet future customer requirements is foundational to thrive. Each of us needs to take personal responsibility and can't rely solely on company paid learning.

As internal auditors, we have nearly unrivaled access to company resources and information. We interface with all facets of the enterprise. Are we able to leverage the full benefits of all this information? Are we equipped with the skills necessary to wade through the white noise to identify and deliver value? Do we have a conscious and systematic talent model to create value? Only recruiting talent from traditional disciplines, such as Accounting and Finance, may not support generation of value in the future. Customer requirements are changing and the profession needs to proactively respond by broadening its perspective. Greater emphasis should be placed on areas of study that employ both creative and critical thinking. Artificial intelligence will continue to replace simplistic analysis and traditional work.

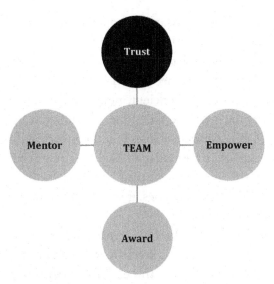

Trust

Early in my career, just after the Sarbanes–Oxley Act passed, the head of the financial reporting organization handpicked me to participate on the company team to implement the new requirements. This was a big deal and a highly visible assignment. It was also my first big lesson in trust. I was unaware of a long-standing strain between the heads of financial reporting and internal audit. Little did I know that I was about to become an unwitting player in the dynamic. I deeply respected both leaders. Turf wars broke out over the project. While I was still officially reporting to the head of internal audit, my time was fully committed to the project, working directly for the head of financial reporting. Both leaders were lobbying, unsuccessfully, for information on the other. It was uncomfortable. One day, as I had been doing regularly, I pulled together a presentation on the project's status to be shared with the CEO. I had a lapse in judgment at that moment. Some of the language in the presentation may have been perceived as unfavorable to internal audit, and I shared it with my boss for fear she would be surprised in the meeting with the CEO. As I should have anticipated, she called the head of financial reporting, incensed. While I was trying to do the right thing, I went about it the wrong way, and in the process, diminished the hard-won trust I had cultivated. The financial reporting director said "Dan, I need to be able to trust you." It was a rookie mistake. I wasn't equipped with the political skills necessary to properly navigate the situation. In hindsight, I should have had the courage to raise my concern directly with him. I didn't appreciate the dynamic that existed between the two, and a matter that seemed smallish in my eyes, was a big deal to him. I was technically proficient, motivated, and a top performer, yet my political inexperience failed me. Fortunately, because we had a good relationship, we were able to rebuild our trust. This experience highlights the critical importance of having strong relationships with our customers, the management team, and the Audit Committee. If we mess up, which everyone does at some point, our relationship can transcend individual events.

Ethics investigation results. Salary information. Pending company acquisitions. Internal audit has access to a vast amount of confidential information. Trust is critical. The executive team understands that internal audit has a duty to provide the Audit Committee insight on the risk environment. This creates a natural tension regarding information exchange. Most internal audit charters require unfettered access to company information. But charter requirements don't necessarily equate with management being forthright or proactive when trouble arises, especially if trust has not been established. We need to take the first steps to establish and demonstrate trust. It takes time, significant effort, and can be a bumpy ride. Like I did, misjudgments will be made. We need to acknowledge setbacks and learn from our mistakes. We also need to be resilient and not let failures hinder progress. Failures, after all, can be the source of our greatest lessons.

Team members should be equipped with the information necessary to do their jobs. Some team members will inadvertently disclose sensitive information. If this happens, use it as a chance for coaching and mentoring. Provide the team member with another opportunity to demonstrate trust. Wash, rinse, and repeat. If a pattern emerges, you've helped the organization identify someone that should be moved to another opportunity. This may seem harsh, but it's critical to have confidence in team members. The earlier that trust is established, the sooner team members can focus on delivering value. In the worst-case scenario, an inexperienced team member may disclose sensitive company information for personal gain. Whistleblower protections are expanding and now include financial rewards for reporting fraudulent activity at publicly traded companies. Securities and Exchange Commission and Dodd–Frank whistleblower protections do not require proof of fraud, just reasonable suspicion. The best thing we can do is create an environment where team members feel safe to report concerns within the chain of command and demonstrate sincere action when warranted. It is particularly important for internal audit management to be approachable.

The Institute of Internal Auditor's Code of Ethics states "The integrity of internal auditors establishes trust and thus provides the basis for reliance on their judgment." The code goes on to state that "Internal auditors respect the value and ownership of information they receive and do not disclose information without appropriate authority unless there is a legal or professional obligation to do so." Further, regarding confidentiality, the code states that internal auditors "shall be prudent in the use and protection of information acquired in the course of their duties" and "shall not use information for any personal gain or in any manner that would be contrary to the law or detrimental to the legitimate and ethical objectives of the organization." Trust is not possible without maturity. We've all seen a staff member that was naïve, power-hungry, or narcissistic.

A colleague at a conference shared the story of an early-career staff auditor who bad-mouthed leadership and fellow team members, bullied customers, and manipulated coworkers. They undermined the company's trust in internal audit and did so willfully. The lack of trust dragged down team morale. The auditor was terminated. Almost immediately, team morale, customer relationships, and organizational performance improved.

In his book, *Trusted Advisors*,[1] Richard Chambers, President and CEO of the Institute of Internal Auditors, talks about the need for "ethical resilience." He broke this resilience down into five factors: integrity, courage, honesty, accountability, and, yes, trustworthiness. He defines trustworthiness as "building a history of ethical behavior that forms a foundation upon which people can place their trust."

Going back to my point on early career mishaps, if you've formed a trusting relationship with your customers, leaders, and Audit Committee, minor mistakes will be overlooked. On the other hand, not having developed trust can create grave circumstances when mistakes occur. Trust, even at the individual level, is critical to the internal audit organization. It can take just one untrustworthy person to damage leadership's confidence in internal audit.

Leadership Responsibility for Developing Trust

Audit management should collaborate with team members to develop expectations. Trust cannot be established, if ground rules have not been agreed upon. Clearly stating expectations and protocols for personal conduct is critical. Many auditors, especially early-career team members, are not going to have deep experience navigating the political environment. It's crucial for the CAE and audit management team to redirect more sensitive matters to audit management and not place early-career auditors in unintentional dilemmas.

Have an open-door policy, allowing team members to seek advice when necessary. It's important for supervisors and managers to be accessible given the myriad of sensitive issues internal auditors can encounter. We never want a team member to feel alone in maneuvering a complex organizational environment. Being mindful that each person will seek help in different ways. Audit management needs to be keenly aware of individual team member signals for help. Human behavior varies widely—some people will be direct and ask for help—others may withdraw signaling discomfort—others may act out demonstrating frustration or to deflect the real challenge at hand.

Provide constructive feedback regularly, highlighting positives and opportunities, linked to expectations. A proactive feedback process builds trust in the team member–leadership relationship. Iterate on prior discussion topics with specific targeted outcomes. Ask the team member what they need to be successful.

Walk the talk and role model positive behaviors for the team. Walking the talk means demonstrating through your own behavior, by example, what you've communicated as important. Every organization has its own culture. If dressing formally is expected, demonstrate that for the team. Avoid creating double standards, which quickly become a source of resentment. Survey the team about what they think reflects positive behaviors for the organization and develop a team pact. Recognize team members that follow-through on the behaviors and provide incentives.

Encourage feedback on obstacles to team success. Literally ask the question—"Is there anything that is making your current role difficult and how can I help?" Structure the solicitation of bad news into categories: process, people, resources and tools, and leadership. Ask about each one regularly and ensure that it's understood that not every piece of bad news will be acted upon. Likewise, ask about what is working and how the organization can leverage positives. Ask about the top three things that each team member values in the current work environment. Ask how they'd rate their job satisfaction on a scale of 1–10 (ten being exceptionally happy) and explore the reasoning for the rating. Compare these ratings over time (quarterly) for changes. Evaluate common themes to be addressed.

Care about the team and individuals. People are more than their occupation. Respect the person and their circumstances. Personal situations can lead to unintended complications in the workplace. Offer team members support and resources when asked. Most of us spend more awake time with our coworkers than anyone else. Having a genuine relationship builds trust.

Be straight with the team member when performance is not meeting expectations and collaborate on a get-well plan. The worst thing we can do is mislead talent about their performance and create an unrealistic view of the situation. Having a clearly defined competency model provides a framework for feedback and objective performance discussions.

Team Member Responsibilities for Developing Trust

Individual team members should provide input for expectations, anticipating personal challenges. Validate understanding of expectations and ask clarifying questions. Ask what success looks like in order to translate the hypothetical into reality. Don't keep your success levers a secret from management. Let them know what gets you excited about work. The management team may not be able to accommodate every individual preference, but it allows them the opportunity to consider possibilities. Management is only as effective as the team, and they want talent to be happy, challenged, and successful.

Properly protect sensitive information. Internal auditors of all experience levels need to appreciate that protecting confidential information is critical to trust. Never hesitate to ask management when there is uncertainty about the right course of action regarding information requests. External and internal stakeholders may intentionally or unwittingly ask for confidential information because they know internal audit has unfettered access.

Respect boundaries. Team members should work with the management team to understand expectations around work–life balance. We read a lot about managers not respecting the work–life balance of their team members, and that can be a significant issue for retaining talent. Likewise, team members should also consider the work–life balance of their management team. Your manager will surely appreciate you putting in extra time after hours or on the weekends, but is it necessary to send a review request on the weekend? Team members should discern what is critical—needing immediate attention—and what can wait until Monday during normal business hours. Audit management is likely already responding to requests from the executive team, and nonurgent matters from the team can diminish trust and respect. The best course of action is to proactively discuss when it's appropriate to communicate off-business hours.

It's also important to remember that management is vested in your success. When they extend trust, team members should make sure to show respect and not take advantage of the situation. A good leader treats the team as professionals—allowing a certain amount of autonomy to complete their work without being micromanaged. However, missing deadlines, showing up late for important meetings, and taking excess time off at inopportune times will quickly ebb the view of the relationship.

Unlimited time off is trending in Silicon Valley. There is an implicit understanding that unlimited time off does not equate with not working or taking long periods of time off during critical delivery periods. In the unlimited time off scenario, team members also understand that if they are on vacation, someone else is stepping in, so it's a matter of trust and respect for colleagues too.

Developing trust means regularly checking in with the team leader. It's important for audit management to schedule regular time for one-on-one meetings. It's equally important to proactively check-in if this is not happening and help management help you. Concerns or roadblocks should be discussed along with potential solutions. A team member who critically thinks through a problem and provides potential solutions will be valued.

Deliver on promises, and when shortfalls occur, ask for guidance on how to improve and be open to feedback. Be honest about difficulties encountered. When mistakes occur, ask for help. Be truthful. Be genuine, learn from the difficulty, and adjust.

Demonstrate integrity with fellow team members, customers, and the audit leader. A prosperous and successful team feeds on positive interaction and behaviors. If John consistently under contributes that affects team morale. Remember the college group project where everyone agreed to distribute the work evenly and there was a collective grade for the paper submitted? Some people haven't overcome being the slacker in the group project, and this raises resentment. No one wants be the slacker. On the flip side of the coin, temper the need to always seek the spotlight and share the credit when the team is successful. Help teammates if they're struggling to complete a specific task. Author Travis Bradberry wrote, "More than half of people who leave their jobs do so because of their relationship with their boss. Smart companies make certain their managers know how to balance being professional with being human. These are the bosses who celebrate an employee's success, empathize with those going through hard times, and challenge people, even when it hurts."

Exhibit 3.1 Trust ladder.

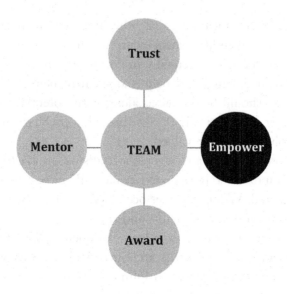

Empower

The Institute of Internal Auditor's 2015 GAIN Survey indicated the average auditor in the United States receives 62 hours of training. The business environment changes faster than the shelf life of milk in your refrigerator. Sixty-two hours is hardly enough training to keep up. Forward thinking internal audit organizations empower team members with knowledge but also investment in company paid learning, assignments to challenging projects, business travel experiences, and tailored learning. Investing in talent increases value to the enterprise and supports customer success.

Learning should be core to the job, continuous, and timely. Dedicating time each week to learning addresses immediate customer needs. Knowledge is more easily retained. Remember learning comes in many forms—not just costly external conferences. There is a wealth of online education available. Lynda.com is just one of many good sources. Many platforms offer learning on a variety of subjects—not just auditing. If we're to add value and understand our customer's business, we need to be at least partly fluent on a variety of subjects.

An approach I've used successfully involves holding a series of weekly lunch-and-learns, two hours at a time, where the team discusses concepts and tools, and collectively performs an exercise. Team members share their struggles and solutions. While there is a facilitator, the real value is in the discussions. An individual team member may lead the session.

So, the team is learning about a particular topic, and one or more team members are also practicing communication and facilitation skills. Researching and preparing to deliver a training on a subject requires greater depth of understanding and embeds the knowledge. A final benefit is mentally shifting the responsibility for learning from company-delivered solutions to team member ownership and empowerment.

The application of learning is another challenge. We've all attended conferences, sitting through a particularly stimulating workshop and jotting down notes and takeaways. What happens next? How do we leverage this information to have an impact? A good practice is to dedicate 30 minutes at the end of each day and assess how what you've learned can be used to advance the value of internal audit's work. Create a personal action plan. Break the learning down into themes—doing so embeds the knowledge and forces a thoughtful process about how the new information relates to your work.

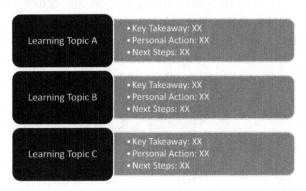

Exhibit 3.2 Learning personal action plan.

Share the learning at your next team meeting. Spreading awareness increases the odds that the information will be leveraged. Is there something from the conference that might interest a customer? Why not draft an email after the day's workshop to the customer outlining the key takeaway and how it might benefit them? This demonstrates caring and reinforces customer commitment. For example, during a recent conference, I sent a short blurb to our corporate controller about developments in Robotic Process Automation. The email offered a personal follow-up with more detail.

A 2015 US Government Accountability Office report indicated that 40% of the US workforce is now contingent labor. This is expected to continue to increase. Each of us is personally responsible for staying relevant and investing in ourselves. Consider artificial intelligence. Going back to the Oxford Martin School study, which predicted that 47% of US jobs would be lost to automation within 10–20 years, combined with contingent labor trends, puts more pressure on each of us to stay relevant.

Empowering Team Members is about Describing Success

Value-added internal audit organizations create competency models linked to company strategic objectives, empowering talent to be successful in the specific environment. Training programs are aligned with the competency model. Individual team members self-assess based on the competency criteria, rating themselves on a scale of "strong," "sufficient," or "opportunity." Items that are rated "strong" and "sufficient" may warrant training if there are significant changes expected in the environment. Competencies rated "opportunity" are prioritized.

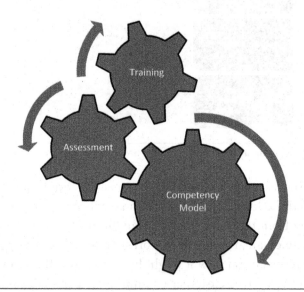

Exhibit 3.3 Empowerment cycle.

Team members perform a self-assessment each time the competency model changes. The training program is then updated. Self-assessments are performed throughout the year, as needed.

Building a Competency Model

The competency model is designed to reflect the company environment. Consider the following:
Strategic objectives

- What are the company's strategic objectives?
- How do the objectives relate to internal audit's mission? Translate each objective into internal audit goals.
- What skills are necessary to achieve those goals?
- How will performance against those goals be measured?
- What behaviors demonstrate success?

Technical ability

- What technical abilities are necessary to support goals and objectives? Consider skills in audit technique, critical thinking, information systems, process improvement, and data analysis. Pay special attention to industry and company-specific skills that support strategic objectives (e.g., manufacturing).
- What type of job experience is required? Who will the audit team be interacting with? If the company is an engineering firm, will engineering expertise help the audit team assess engineering processes? If it is a healthcare company, will experience in evaluating healthcare systems be important? If the company works with government, will government experience be essential?
- What behaviors demonstrate technical competence?

Leadership

- What leadership qualities enable success at the company? Is it a command and control organization or a collaborative environment?
- How is honesty and integrity demonstrated at the company?
- How is reliability and dependability demonstrated?
- How is courage exhibited?
- Does the company culture encourage calculated risk taking (ethical risk taking)?
- What behaviors reflect transparency?
- How can auditors demonstrate accountability?

Communication and influencing

- How do successful people and teams communicate at the company?
- How is change influenced?
- How do facilitators manage change?
- What writing skills are necessary?
- What presentation skills are necessary?

Professional knowledge

- What professional certifications are needed? Consider the usual, such as Certified Internal Auditor, Certified Public Accountant, Certified Information Systems Auditor, but also nontraditional certifications such as Project Management Professional Certification.

People/teaming

- What types of coaches and mentors would be helpful to encourage and accelerate talent growth?
- How does the company recognize individual and team success? Translate to team behaviors.
- How is organizational capability grown?
- How is talent identified?

Exhibit 3.4 Competency Model Example

COMPETENCY	COMPETENCY DESCRIPTION	BEHAVIORS (AUDITOR)
Company environment	Understands and communicates company's mission, vision, strategies, and goals.	• Uses market, industry, and benchmarking knowledge to identify new opportunities to add value. • Builds cooperation between departments and teams. • Responds quickly to changing situations.
Technical ability	Applies appropriate technical skills to assess problems.	• Effectively documents workflows and identifies value-add opportunities. • Employs data analytics effectively. • Understands Committee of Sponsoring Organizations (COSO)-based controls design.
Leadership	Understand how to get things done in the environment.	• Ensures customer's trust in internal audit. • Dedicated to establishing and maintaining effective relationships. • Delivers value to ensure customer success.

(Continued)

Exhibit 3.4 (*Continued*) Competency Model Example

COMPETENCY	COMPETENCY DESCRIPTION	BEHAVIORS (AUDITOR)
Communication and influencing	Ability to communicate and influence effectively based on the immediate circumstances.	• Communicates relevant information clearly and succinctly. • Conveys ideas with the power to inspire people to action. • Listens actively to understand.
Professional knowledge	Has the requisite professional knowledge to perform the job and add value for the customer.	• Understands the International Professional Practices Framework of the Institute of Internal Auditors. • Applies applicable control frameworks: COSO, Control Objectives for Information and Related Technologies (COBIT), Enterprise Risk Management (ERM). • Demonstrates understanding of applicable industry-specific concepts.
People/teaming	Can work successfully with various personality types both individually and in group settings.	• Promotes a professional and cooperative climate, including respecting confidentiality. • Demonstrates the ability to adapt personal style to accommodate differences. • Earns/inspires the trust of others.

Career Planning

According to the US Bureau of Labor Statistics, newly hired millennials stay on the job an average of two years. How can we effectively add value when team members leave so quickly?

Developing a career plan can improve retention while also empowering team members to take charge of their career path. Career planning empowers success, demonstrates caring, broadcasts opportunities for growth, and facilitates a discussion about the future. Seeking different work experiences every 2–5 years keeps talent refreshed. Team members should consider company assignments inside and outside internal audit. Rotations to other regions and offices can create new paths for development and advancement.

I've mentored a number of internal auditors who have become CAEs, financial controllers, program managers, and entrepreneurs. They've cited the impact that career planning had on their success. Many are still working at their first company, working through numerous roles, which kept them challenged and engaged.

Start with career interests. Working with the team member, understand and document short-term (one year), near-term (three years), and long-term (five+ years) interests.

- What internal audit projects/opportunities would the team member like to pursue this year?
  - Does the team member want to remain in internal audit near term or rotate to a different role?
  - Identify roles and positions outside of internal audit that are realistic possibilities.
  - Does the company have a rotation program? If so, is the team member eligible to participate in the program? Document rotation program opportunities.
- What internal audit roles would the team member like to pursue near term? For example, would the team member like to become an audit manager?
- What non-audit roles would the team member like to pursue near term? Are these roles available within the company?
- What longer term roles would the team member like to pursue? Can the organization support this given staffing and succession planning?

Create a development plan. Identify gaps based on the internal audit competency model. Now consider competency models for the target role and document skill gaps. Identify work experiences, learning, and mentoring that would address the gaps.

- Are there projects that would provide on-the-job learning?
- Are there volunteer opportunities to develop leadership skills?

Career Planning Matrix

Career Interests	Development Plan
• List near and long-term potential career interests. • List sponsor / champion. • Meet with people currently in position/s identified.	• Note competency model. • Document skills gaps. • List mentors that can help with specific learning. • List non-job-related opportunities to develop leadership skills.
Personal Brand	**Training / Networking**
• Write personal brand statement / vision. • Document current brand based on peer feedback (e.g. 360 assessment)	• Document learning plan to address competency gaps. • Document goals of mentoring relationship.

Exhibit 3.5   Career planning matrix.

Co-sourcing

Internal audit work is becoming increasingly dynamic to respond to the changing business environment. Empowering team success may include co-sourcing to meet customer needs or to complement existing talent. Co-sourcing provides flexibility. Instead of hiring a full-time employee, co-sourced talent can step in when staffing needs arise.

Co-sourcing provides the team with an outside perspective on how to perform a specific audit.

Consider a co-sourcing solution when the following conditions exist:

- The internal audit organization is being established for the first time. Co-source partners can provide insights to leading practices.
- There is a need for information technology capability not currently available on the team. Smaller internal audit organizations may not have a full-time information technology auditor.
- The company is undergoing a major transition, and additional audit resources are needed to evaluate the changing functions, systems, and processes.
- The company has overseas or remote operations, where specific language or cultural skills are necessary.
- The company is rapidly expanding into a new market and existing auditor expertise does not match needs. For instance, acquiring a business in a different industry.

I like to use co-sourcing solutions for subject-matter expertise. External providers with deep knowledge on information security, specific regulations, and industry can provide real value. What does this have to do with internal talent and empowering the team? Every effort includes interaction with our team members and knowledge transfer from the subject-matter expert. These arrangements also normally include access to the service provider's research or "thought leadership" group. It's another form of training. Recalling the Chinese proverb, "If you want one year of prosperity, grow grain. If you want 10 years of prosperity, grow trees. If you want 100 years of prosperity, grow people."

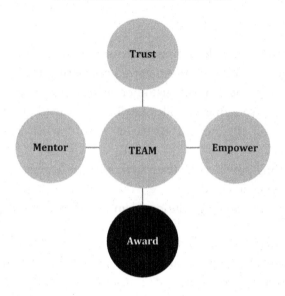

Award (and Reward)

Creating high-performing teams means recognizing and awarding (rewarding) achievements. The team is an extension of the internal audit brand. The greater the team's success, the more positive the perception of internal audit. Smart leaders find creative ways to acknowledge team members. They personalize rewards. Cash bonuses that are important to one team member may be less valuable to another.

Ask team members and customers to nominate individuals for recognition. Link awards to value provided by the internal audit team. Team members that receive positive feedback from customers should be recognized.

Celebrate team successes by holding an office party or off-site event. Teams that play well together, work well together. After long projects, reserve time for the team to have fun and recognize their success. I've taken teams bowling, to sporting events, to amusement parks, apple and pumpkin picking, and to theatrical shows, like BlueMan Group. Awards come in many forms—recognition, financial rewards, and promotions. An impactful recognition can be simply saying "thank you."

Consider intervals when designing awards for team members:

- Real-time, spot recognition. Recognize the team member in the moment for an effective presentation, completion of an audit, interaction with a customer.

- Weekly, monthly, or quarterly recognition associated with organizational meetings. Ask team members to highlight another team member for a job well done.
- Annual awards for best performances. For example, dedicate an award to a competency model category, such as Technical Ability, and recognize the individual or team that best exemplifies the qualities for that competency.

Budget funds for team members to provide awards to other team members.

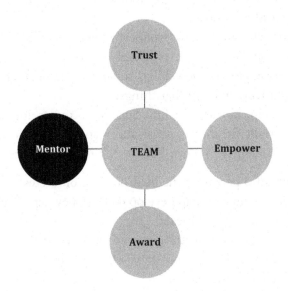

Mentoring

Do you have a mentor? Do you mentor others?

Early in my career, I received a phone call at 2 AM on a Saturday in Britain, at the end of a grueling four week international audit, working 80 hour weeks. I was flying home the next day. The person on the other line was my supervisor, who was back in the United States. He was angry, threatening and fuming as to why we hadn't performed certain work that was never part of the scope, and wanted to know how I could let this happen. The boss said that "someone" might be fired.

How would you respond? Would you be upset? Would you keep your calm? I kept my composure and offered several solutions to address the issue, despite being half-awake.

My mentor at the time shared her life experience with similar bosses. Note that I use the term boss. A boss is bossy. A leader leads. A manager manages. The person on the other line that night was being bossy and not helping solve a problem as a leader.

My mentor shared that we are always being evaluated by our colleagues, our customers, and our leadership when things are going well and not so well. Life is full of difficult people.

The experience helped develop resilience. It taught me how not to treat team members. To this day, that phone call and my mentor's guidance are etched in my mind and a reminder about how to be a "leader" instead of a "boss."

I've been fortunate to have wonderful mentors. They've been supportive and candid. They've provided constructive feedback about leadership style, presentation skills, career development, and relationship management, among other things.

Mentors help us translate life. Successful mentoring starts with finding the right fit, mutual trust and respect, predefined expectations, and availability to meet. When seeking a mentor consider

- A successful person in the field/position of interest.
- Someone who can help develop competency gaps, whether it be leadership or technical.
- A person with a different perspective/life experience.
- Someone who has demonstrated effective coaching.
- Comfort with the person.
- Limiting to no more than two to three mentors at a time.

The following ground rules support a mutually productive mentoring relationship.

Mentees should

- Be open to feedback and willing to learn.
- Be prepared for mentoring sessions and respect the mentor's time.
- Dedicate time outside of the mentoring meetings to do independent learning.
- Be trustworthy and keep mentoring discussions in confidence.
- Demonstrate maturity, professionalism, and a positive attitude during mentoring sessions.

- Ask good questions/be inquisitive.
- Identify how to add value for the mentor. For instance, reverse mentor perspectives.
- Respect boundaries.
- Evaluate progress.

Mentors should

- Provide feedback in a constructive manner. Avoid judgments.
- Establish short- and long-term goals for the mentoring relationship.
- Provide recommendations for personal learning.
- Be willing to share life experiences including difficult challenges.
- Model behavior.
- Initiate important discussions.
- Make every mentoring session/discussion valuable for the mentee.
- Agree on boundaries.
- Evaluate progress.

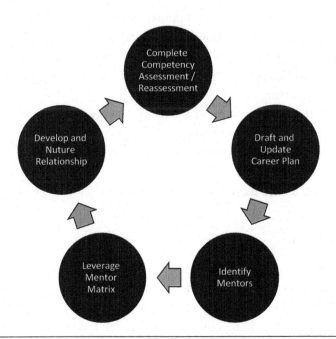

 Exhibit 3.6 Mentoring life cycle.

The team member/team leader relationship is an important mentoring opportunity. Going back to empowerment, team leader mentoring improves performance, helps goal achievement, and increases job satisfaction. When delivering feedback, the team leader should use it as part of a larger mentoring feedback loop. Real-time feedback is becoming increasingly important.

A 2015 TriNet and Wakefield Research study indicated that millennials, who now make up the largest generational share of the workforce, would like more frequent conversations on performance. The results showed that the quality of the conversation was important, with 32% of study participants wanting more open dialogue.

The need for open, high-quality performance discussions aligns with a mentoring approach to feedback. Providing real-time feedback in the context of career planning focuses the discussion on team member success. Consider the following when providing feedback:

- Highlight positive performance. Be specific.
- Relate feedback to the competency model and career plan.
- Keep the feedback conversational. Ask how the team member thought X went.
- Sandwich improvement opportunities with positive points. For instance, "I like how you facilitated the conversation with John Doe. Do you think there is anything we could do differently to better meet his expectations? Thanks for your efforts in supporting our customers."
- Ask how you can support the team member or if other support would be helpful.
- Develop next steps together to improve performance including specific goals.
- Set up a time for a follow-up discussion within 30 days.

Chapter Recap

- Create a trust framework for the team.
- Empower the team with the knowledge, training, and experiences necessary to support success.
- Implement a core competency model based on company needs.

- Collaborate with team members to develop a career plan.
- Leverage co-sourcing to complement team skills and respond to temporary staffing needs.
- Celebrate team and individual success and provide financial and nonfinancial awards.
- Establish a mentoring framework.
- Encourage and support team members in finding mentors to fill gaps associated with the core competency model and career plan.

Notes

1 Richard F. Chambers, Trusted Advisers: Key Attributes of Outstanding Internal Auditors, page 17. Internal Audit Foundation, January 31, 2017.

Bibliography

Malcolm Gladwell, Outliers: The Story of Success, Little, Brown and Company (November 18, 2008).

Institute of Internal Auditor's 2015 GAIN Survey.

2015 TriNet and Wakefield Research Study, www.trinet.com/about-us/news-press/press-releases/survey-performance-reviews-drive-one-in-four-millennials-to-search-for-a-new-job-or-call-in-sick.

US Bureau of Labor Statistics. https://www.bls.gov/news.release/tenure.nr0.htm

2015 US Government Accountability Office. https://www.gao.gov/assets/670/669766.pdf

World Economic Forum 2015 Technological Tipping Points Survey, www3.weforum.org/docs/WEF_GAC15_Technological_Tipping_Points_report_2015.pdf.

FACTOR 4
RISK EXPERTISE

There had been a few odd instances of dogs collapsing and dying during walks with their owners in New York City. At first it seemed like a fluke, perhaps the dogs were overheated. The owners didn't give it much thought. Then January 16, 2004, happened. A woman was out with her two dogs, when they suddenly and inexplicably started to attack each other. The owner reached down to calm the dogs, when she collapsed and went into cardiac arrest. She later died.[1] ConEdison, a company founded in 1823 and a well-respected institution, acknowledged that the woman died after stepping on a metal plate that had become electrified by a wire inside of a poorly insulated utility box. The company settled with the woman's family for $7.2 million and agreed to establish an electrical safety committee, which included two representatives from the victim's family.[2] The events resulted in public and regulatory scrutiny of its operations, which would later come back to haunt them. Matters got worse, when on November 22, 2011, fourteen ConEdison supervisors were found guilty of bribery for seeking $1 million in kickbacks from contractors making repairs.[3] The Public Service Commission found that the company had not properly supervised its employees. ConEdison settled with the Commission and paid back $170 million to its customers. The electric distribution and bribery issues were followed by a tragic gas explosion in March 2014, which killed eight people and injured 50. As a result, new regulatory oversight was implemented, and the company paid damages of $153 million.[4] In all, nine people, all customers, were dead, 50 were injured, and $330 million in damages were paid.

In the bribery case, the Public Service Commission noted that there was a breakdown in communication of information between internal audit and ConEdison's security services.[5] Then in 2012, ConEdison moved the Business Ethics and Compliance group from internal audit to the Legal Department. Now, imagine if the internal audit department had been able to provide prospective insight on the totality of the company's risk. Consider (1) electric and gas distribution systems in the northeastern United States were first installed in the early 1900s, so they are aged; a known risk. (2) ConEdison's service territory is huge with 93,000 miles of underground cable and 7,200 miles of gas pipes,[6] prioritizing maintenance must surely be complex. (3) Replacement of these systems is costly because they are buried below street surfaces, and as time passes, the electric lines become less accessible, all the while profitability pressures remain. (4) New York has seen significant construction projects in the last 30 years, transforming the skyline. Various contractors complete these projects, which involve digging up street surfaces, creating exposure to the utility's infrastructure. (5) The company employs over 13,000 people, presenting significant potential work performance variation. (6) New York has a history of perceived corruption. Research by Dr. Jeffrey Milyo of the University of Missouri ranked New York as #1 in public corruption cases.

Each of these risks is individually significant, but taken together it becomes substantial. Did the company understand how its work culture could influence the potential for bribery, which could affect the quality of contractor maintenance? Was there an appreciation for heightened risk between the age of infrastructure and where construction work was occurring? Did the company use data regarding infrastructure failure rates and age of assets to forecast where maintenance should be proactively performed? Internal audit can provide significant value by connecting the dots on risk for management and helping them to identify blind spots.

Internal audit has unfettered access to information, resources, and people, which coupled with its unique qualifications, positions it as a prime expert for providing insight. Others with risk expertise may have a limited scope or constrained access to information. Every internal auditor is a sensor, working to sniff out potential risks for functional owners, the executive team, and Audit Committee members.

In many ways, internal audit's prime responsibility is to be risk experts. It's not possible to achieve our goal of providing assurance without also having a complete understanding of risks. The International Standards for the Professional Practice of Internal

Auditing (The Standards) states, "The internal audit activity adds value to the organization and its stakeholders when it considers strategies, objectives, and risks; strives to offer ways to enhance governance, risk management, and control processes; and objectively provides relevant assurance."[7]

At the end of the day, companies and process owners are looking to meet their objectives, which requires identifying and addressing risks that prevent achieving those objectives. The Standards also state, "When assisting management in establishing or improving risk management processes, internal auditors must refrain from assuming any management responsibility by actually managing risks."[8] So, there is a fine line for us to follow between leading risk awareness and managing risks.

To truly add value, we need to lead on risk awareness, understanding, and action. This chapter will outline the ways in which internal audit can be the company's risk expert. There are many books written about risk assessments, monitoring, and mitigation. The Committee of Sponsoring Organizations (COSO) has an excellent framework for implementing Enterprise Risk Management. The following is intended to highlight ways in which internal audit can have a practical and immediate impact at improving management's understanding of company risks.

Understanding Risk

A risk is anything that prevents the achievement of an objective. It covers strategy, operations, reporting, and compliance. Risks are ever present, continuously evolve, and have varying velocity. They are present at the highest level of an entity with broad potential impact, down to the individual worker striving to fulfill responsibilities. Risks are interdependent, driving complexity. Too often, risks are viewed in silos. For instance, two lower levels risks may drive the likelihood of other negative events occurring, creating a higher overall risk. An individual high or critical risk that management is comfortable accepting may be unacceptable when married with another high or critical risk. The realization of one risk may increase the likelihood that other risks will occur. Internal audit needs to help management make connections between risks and overall risk levels.

For example, the government of Japan is well aware of the risk to its citizens of seismic activity. Japan is located on the so-called Ring of Fire, the most active seismic area of the world. The government likely had response plans in place to address the aftermath of a significant earthquake. However, did they consider the risk posed by a major tsunami to infrastructure as a consequence of a major earthquake? The government also likely considered the impact of its nuclear reactors melting down. What they may not have considered was how seismic risk, tsunami risk, and nuclear waste risk could be related. The earthquake increased the risk of a tsunami, which in turn increased the risk of nuclear disaster.

Risk Likelihood

Risk likelihood is the probability that a risk will be realized. It's normal to see organizations rate likelihood on a scale of 1–3 or 1–5. The higher the score, the more likely the risk will occur. Internal audit needs to help management think about likelihood. Low likelihood may represent a 0%–25% chance of occurrence. High likelihood may represent a risk that has been realized in the recent past or one that has a 75% chance of occurring. But how do we consider whether something is likely to occur?

What's often not considered is how one risk increases the likelihood of another risk. If Risk A inherently has a low likelihood of occurring, management may not dedicate resources to address it. However, what happens when Risk A is influenced by Risk B, so when Risk B occurs, Risk A is almost certain to occur? Management then doesn't have a full understanding of both Risks A and B and their combined potential impact.

Imagine a situation where talent recruitment and retention are rated as a high likelihood risk. In other words, a company may not be able to recruit and retain the talent it needs to fulfill its objectives. If management considers this risk in a vacuum, it may be comfortable accepting some of this risk. However, if we couple that with another risk, such as cyber security, it creates a different perspective. Let's say that the risk of a cyber attack has a high likelihood. Management may have little appetite for a successful cyberattack and therefore commits significant resources to reduce the likelihood of it occurring. What may not be appreciated is the linkage between the ability to recruit and retain information security talent and the ability to defend against a cyberattack. Taking cyber risk into account, the talent recruitment and retention risk becomes more significant, and management may want to invest more resources to address talent.

Risk Impact

Impact is the effect that a risk has on the business when realized. Impact can be difficult to determine. Some organizations religiously translate risk in terms of potential financial impact, while others are more subjective in their evaluation. Materiality for risk is typically tied to some financial metric, such as assets or net income. The specific measure will depend on the business being evaluated.

Risk Velocity

Velocity is the speed with which risk manifests. In other words, is the risk likely to occur sooner rather than later? It's an important consideration when determining whether scarce resources should be applied to mitigate risk. If the risk is not expected to be realized in the near future, it may be wise to take a measured approach to resolution. If the risk is expected to accelerate and is more likely to occur soon, it provides management with a sense of urgency.

For example, the US government has been funding agencies and contractors through a series of continuing resolutions. Comparing this risk to a new regulatory requirement may seem to have similar risk profiles based on the likelihood vs. impact assessment. However, considering velocity, a government shutdown may take effect with little warning and a near certainty of it happening. A new government regulation might have a low velocity, as the regulatory drafting process is slow with ample time to prepare and respond. Velocity, therefore, provides management with additional context for the risk and how urgently it may need to be mitigated, thus helping to prioritize resources.

Risk Influencers

Risk influencers are factors that drive the overall severity of a risk. It's the internal and external forces that push and pull in determining whether a risk will come to fruition and how severe the impact will be. Internal risk influencers can be the maturity of controls that are in place, which can reduce a higher, inherent risk, to a lower, residual risk. Or it can be an external factor that is difficult to measure or an unknown, increasing the overall residual risk level. When thinking about risk influencers, consider the following questions:

- How well understood is the risk? Are there many unknowns?
- How much of the risk does management control vs. external forces?
- How mature are the processes and controls addressing the risk? Are the controls manual or automated?
- Is the risk dynamic?
- Have there been or will there be major changes to risk ownership?
- Has there been employee turnover in the areas associated with the risk?
- Are significant system or process changes planned that will affect the risk?
- Are regulations related to this risk evolving, becoming more or less burdensome, or becoming more or less complex?
- How good is the quality of data related to the risk?
- Are there positive potential upsides to the risk?
- How does the company culture influence whether the risk will be addressed?
- Have there been any Black Swan Events involving other companies in the industry?

Risk occurs at all levels of an enterprise from asteroid sized risks that could shut down a business to those that would prevent an individual from meeting their goals. Internal audit can provide value at every level of risk identification, assessment, and mitigation.

Mega Risk and Enterprise Risk Management (ERM)

At the top level, internal audit provides value by facilitating identification and assessment of catastrophic risks to an enterprise. Management generally has some level of awareness about those risks and their potential impact. The executive team may not have identified all of them, may not appreciate their significance, or how they relate to other risks. Facilitating a discussion about top risks delivers value.

Unfortunately, companies may only initiate identification of top risks once a major event has occurred. Take the example of Volkswagen, which has undergone government scrutiny and class action lawsuits for its failure to prevent manipulation of software in its cars. One would think that compliance would be on Volkswagen's mega risk list. Yet, perhaps, the executive team failed to identify software manipulation, as a specific and significant compliance risk to address. Volkswagen has incurred several billion dollars to cover losses for misrepresentation of compliance. The company's reputation has been damaged, its value impacted, and individuals are facing prosecution. If software manipulation was on its list of mega risks, perhaps second line of defense functions would more strenuously scrutinize practices and controls.

Chipotle, the quick food provider, has spent several years overcoming public relations and reputation damage from customers becoming sick after eating their food. The episode negatively impacted their stock and earnings. Stores closed. Certainly Chipotle, like most restaurant chains, had a rigorous food safety program, yet the unthinkable still happened and customers got sick. Where was food safety on the company's list of top risks? Was internal audit providing an independent perspective on the likelihood of a negative event?

Identifying Top Risks to the Company

To identify the company's top risks, we first need to understand the strategic objectives. Mature companies will have a strategic plan. Leverage the plan and discussions with C-Suite executives, as appropriate, to identify the strategic objectives. If a strategic plan is not available, meet with the company's top executives to gain insights on major initiatives. These discussions are normally led by the Chief Audit Executive given the sensitivity of the information and individuals involved. A strategy may be in place but not referred to as a "strategic plan."

What is the company looking to accomplish in terms of customers, the market, and its business model? What are the defined financial and operational goals?

The next step is to determine what could prevent objectives from being achieved. Depending on the company culture and executive preferences, this is done through facilitated brainstorming sessions with the executive team, one-on-one interviews, or simply by surveying the executive team via email or an electronic survey tool. The target audience for these questions include the CEO, corporate presidents and/or the Chief Operating Officer, the CFO, General Counsel, business unit presidents, and other C-Suite executives. Conduct advanced research to identify industry-specific concerns and looming regulatory changes. By doing so, the conversation is not just a request for information but also an exchange, delivering potentially new information and value to the executive team.

Capture the following information for each major risk:

- Overall risk title: describes the risk in two or three words.
- Risk description: a more detailed description of the risk including circumstances that make it relevant and the impact of the risk, if it were realized.
- Influencers: factors that are influencing the risk to be more significant.
- Near-term issues: the immediate concerns that management should be addressing related to the risk.
- Management levers and initiatives: actions that management is taking to mitigate the risks. This is a high-level description of the action. A more detailed action plan/s should be documented and tracked separately.
- Suggested audit actions: a description of how the top risk relates to the audit plan or other actions that internal audit may take, such as monitoring of a business activity.

Risk Title	
Brief Description: Risk Interdependencies:	
Influencers	Management Levers / Initiatives
Near Term Issues	Suggested Audit Actions

Exhibit 4.1 Top risk profile.

Now that the top risks have been identified, we need to assess their likelihood of occurrence, impact, and velocity. The culmination of these factors will provide a clearer view of how critical it is to take further actions to mitigate the risk. Leverage the existing information collected on management levers and initiatives as a starting point to identify responsible risk owners. Meet with each risk owner and determine the following:

- What part of the risk does the risk owner have responsibility for? Some risks are complex and involve multiple parties to monitor, control, and mitigate. If there are other owners of the risk, who are they and how are risk management responsibilities shared?
- Is the Enterprise Risk Management (ERM) risk included in the risk owner's goals and objectives? If so, how does the risk owner measure performance against the objective?
- What controls are in place to mitigate the risk? How can the risk owner demonstrate that controls are working effectively? Keep in mind that controls in this context could include projects and major initiatives under way to support meeting the strategic objectives and correspondingly mitigate the risk.
- Are there any efforts underway to further mitigate the risk?
- How much residual risk does the risk owner believe remains once controls are considered? What factors were used in making this determination? How confident is the risk owner in the residual level of risk?
- What are the potential impacts of the risk occurring? Consider operational, financial, and compliance impacts in addition to the inability to meet strategic objectives. How have operational and compliance impacts been assessed? Have all relevant parties within the company been included in the assessment of potential impacts?
- If the risk were to be realized, is it more or less likely to occur in the near term or at a later period of time? What factors were used in making this determination?
- What indicators exist to monitor the risk? What does the risk owner do with this information?

- How does the risk owner communicate significant changes in risk levels to the management team? Are protocols in place to inform management when a change in risk level occurs?
- How does this risk relate to or potentially influence other risks? If this risk occurs, will it trigger other risks to occur? If this risk is fully mitigated, will it reduce the likelihood of another risk from occurring?
- What are the biggest impediments in mitigating the risk?
- Is there a question that we haven't asked that we should? Is there any additional context or information about the risk that we should consider?

Take the inputs from the risk owner and document in a Risk Assessment and Mitigation Plan. There may be multiple risk owner plans if responsibilities are shared.

Total Risk Level (High, High-Med, Medium, Medium-Low, Low)	Risk Assessment and Mitigation Plan for XX	
Description of Controls Control 1: Control 2:	Risk Velocity: High, Medium, Low
Risk Likelihood Inherent Likelihood: High, Medium, Low Residual Likelihood: High, Medium, Low	Risk Indicators Indicator A: Indicator B: Indicator C:
Risk Impact Financial Impact: Operational Impact: Compliance Impact:	Risk Co-owners: Risk Interdependencies:

Exhibit 4.2   Risk assessment and mitigation plan.

The top-level ERM Risk Profile can now be updated to more fully describe the risk and mitigation actions. Work with the executive team to understand the residual risk. Does the executive team want to assume the residual risk, further mitigate it through additional action, or take other measures, for instance insurance, to reduce the exposure for the company? Share risk interdependencies with the executive team for consideration. Risk interdependencies illuminate relationships not previously considered.

Exhibit 4.3 Risk facilitation cycle.

Risk Appetite

Risk appetite is frequently overlooked as a point of discussion. The COSO defines risk appetite as "the amount of risk, on a broad level, an organization is willing to accept in pursuit of value. Each organization pursues various objectives to add value and should broadly understand the risk it is willing to undertake in doing so." Taking zero risk is, therefore, not an option. Businesses look to exploit risk to create opportunities. Internal auditors tend to default to zero risk acceptance. The idea that we can or would want to control for everything is both unwise and a nonstarter for delivering value. Internal auditors need to put on their business hats when articulating risk to management and helping them evaluate potential implications. Internal audit can play an instrumental role in the development of management and the board's risk appetite. From the COSO white paper "Enterprise Risk Management—Understanding and Communicating Risk Appetites,"[9] COSO recommends asking the following questions:

- On a scale of 1–10, with 1 being the lowest, describe what you believe the organization's overall risk appetite has been and what you think it should be. Explain any differences between what you perceive it has been and what you believe it should be. Relate this to your number one strategic goal.
- Various operations help an organization achieve its objectives. Using the categories below, or other categories consistent with the organization's operations, rate the desired risk appetite related to

the following (rating can be broad, such as high, medium, or low, or precise, such as specific metrics that should not be exceeded):

a. Meeting customer requirements
b. Employee health and safety
c. Environmental responsibility
d. Financial reporting
e. Operational performance
f. Regulatory compliance
g. Shareholder expectations
h. Strategic initiatives/growth targets

As you rate each category, indicate areas where you believe the organization is taking either too much or too little risk in pursuing its objectives.

- How would you rate the effectiveness of the organization's process for identifying, assessing, managing, and reporting risks in relation to the overall risk appetite? What are the major areas for improvement?

- Are management's strategies communicated sufficiently for there to be meaningful discussion of risk appetite in pursuit of those strategies, both at the broad organizational level and at the operational level, and for consistency to be analyzed?

- How satisfied are you that the board is providing effective oversight of the risk appetite through its governance process? This includes board committees and/or the board itself to help set the appetite and to monitor over time that management is adhering to the overall risk appetite in pursuit of value.

- Whom do you see as more accepting of risk or more willing to take risks to meet the goals of the organization?
  a. Management
  b. Board
  c. Management and board have similar levels of acceptable risk

- Does the organization motivate management (senior management and operational management) to take higher than desired risks because of the compensation plans in place? If yes, how do you believe the compensation plans should be modified to bring approaches for generating high performance within the risk appetite?

- What do you believe the organization should do?

a. Reduce its risk appetite
b. Increase its risk appetite
c. Make no change
- Do you believe there are risks considered to be above the organization's existing risk appetite that need to be reduced? In other words, are there areas where the risk appetite, as currently used, is too low?
- What risks over the past 5 years were, in your view, above the organization's risk appetite? Were the risks understood when a strategy was developed? How could management have communicated its risk appetite so that the board could both (a) evaluate the risk appetite and (b) provide proper oversight? How could management have communicated its risk appetite so as to hold operational units to actions consistent with the risk appetite?

Who, other than internal audit, raises risk appetite as a point of discussion? The executive team generally has a sense of their risk appetite but may not have thoroughly considered or communicated the appetite to management teams, around the company, responsible for meeting objectives. Each function or business unit needs guidance for how much risk they should accept when pursuing business goals. A high-level risk appetite statement sets the overall expectation. The executive team also needs to translate the risk appetite statement for each company objective. For instance, the executive team may have a very low risk tolerance related to noncompliance with regulations but a higher tolerance for meeting operation efficiencies. Internal audit can be the honest broker in facilitating these discussions and add value. Extend the initial risk appetitive to operationalize risk acceptability at the functional level by helping risk owners translate and develop risk tolerances for their area of responsibility.

Creating a Risk Universe

More broadly, internal audit can add value by working with customers to identify, assess, and help monitor the full Risk Universe for the company. Individual department and function owners have a vested interest in meeting their own objectives and meeting their obligations as the first and second lines of defense. The Risk Universe extends beyond ERM to determine the top risks by major work area (i.e., human resources, finance, information technology, business development, business units, etc.). The Risk Universe will vary by company depending on business activity.

Start by engaging the function/department leader and determining whether functional risks have already been identified. If so, review the assessment with the leader for completeness and verify the assessment results continue to be relevant. If functional risks have not been identified and assessed, partner with the leader to schedule a risk brainstorming workshop. The session should include representation for each major group within the department (e.g., compensation manager within human resources). Obtain the major objectives of the department from the function leader ahead of the workshop and send in a communication to the workshop participants. The first session should include an introduction outlining the purpose of the workshop, basic training on risks and controls, and identification of risks to the objectives. A second workshop with the same team should be scheduled shortly after the first session; generally, within a week. During the second session document the following:

- Likelihood of the risk occurring. Rate on an agreed upon scale (e.g., 1–3 or 1–5)
- Impact of the risk occurring (operational, compliance, financial). Rate on the same scale used to rate likelihood
- Controls in place to mitigate the risk
- Perceived residual risk considering the controls identified Rate on the same scale already used
- Total risk score (residual risk × risk impact)
- Risk velocity (increasing, steady, decreasing)
- Linkage to ERM top risk, if there is one

As we discussed previously, measuring risk impact is somewhat subjective and varies by company. Some companies prefer to adhere to a strict financial interpretation, generally tied to total impact on revenue, net profit, or another relevant metric. A high-risk impact may represent a reduction of 2%–10% of the designated key performance indicator, depending on management's risk appetite. It can quickly become untenable having varying definitions for high, medium, and low impacts. Internal audit can add value by helping to define a company standard. A consistent standard will help compare risks across functions, especially when resource trade-offs must be made.

Exhibit 4.4 Function Risk Landscape Template

FUNCTION NAME:

OBJECTIVE A: BLENDED RISK SCORE: (HIGH, MEDIUM, LOW)

RISK DESCRIPTION	LIKELIHOOD (INHERENT) 1 = LOW 2 = MED 3 = HIGH	LIKELIHOOD (RESIDUAL) 1 = LOW 2 = MED 3 = HIGH	IMPACT 1 = LOW 2 = MED 3 = HIGH	RISK SCORE (RESIDUAL LIKELIHOOD × IMPACT)	RISK VELOCITY (INCREASING, STEADY, DECREASING)	CONTROLS	ERM LINK
Risk A							
Risk B							
Risk C							

The process above can be repeated for each objective within each function across the company. The next step is to determine an overall risk rating for each functional objective. Consider the rating of each individual risk to arrive at a blended risk level. Work with the internal customer to determine the overall risk scale. If there is only one risk for an objective, the rating for that risk becomes the objective rating. Each objective is then entered into the Risk Landscape for the company. This represents a top-level view of risks for each function or business unit.

Company-Wide Risk Dashboard/Landscape Example

I facilitate and maintain a risk dashboard (landscape) which captures all of the major functions and associated significant processes (units). Each process is rated based on residual risk vulnerability and impact. Where there is correlation with a top five risk, it is noted. The dashboard includes management's risk response and approximate recommended audit coverage (annual, biannual, every 3 years, greater than every 3 years). We also include coverage by external parties, such as regulators or external auditors. Brief comments are included, where appropriate, to provide additional context. Separate from the dashboard is the detailed Function Risk Landscape (discussed earlier) associated with each process. The Risk Landscapes are updated on a quarterly basis in conjunction with the risk owners. I also facilitate a quarterly Risk and Compliance Forum with all major risk owners to discuss current and emerging risks to determine whether action is required or if the risks need to be communicated to executive team members. Internal audit leverages the information from the quarterly Risk and Compliance Forum and the dashboard to identify areas requiring immediate attention. The dashboard information supports continuous evaluation of the risk environment.

Company Risk Landscape															
				Risk Type				Residual		Overall	Audit Plan Coverage				
Mega Risk	Ref #	Unit	ERM Link	Compliance	Reporting	Operations	Strategic	Likelihood	Impact	Risk	Annual	Bi-Annual	3 Years	>3 Years	
Accounting	1	AP			X	X									
	2	Billing			X	X									
	3	Fin Close			X										
	4	Fixed Assets			X	X									
	5	Inventory			X	X									
Business Operations	6	XXXX													
	7														
	8														
	9														
	10														
	11														
	12														
	13														
A	B	C	D	E				F	G	H	I				

Exhibit 4.5 Company risk landscape template.

A: This lists the function or mega process from the function risk template

B: Unique reference number, which ties back to the function risk landscape

C: The unit/function evaluated

D: Linkage to the top-level ERM risk assessment

E: The type of risk (compliance, reporting, or operations)

F: The residual risk likelihood rating for the unit

G: The impact of the risk for the unit

H: The overall risk rating for the unit

I: Lists the recommended internal audit coverage for the objective

The Company risk landscape is a concise way to communicate risk levels across all functions, allowing the executive team to more easily monitor risk trends and quickly identify potential concerns.

Risks are classified as one or more of the following types: compliance, financial reporting, operations, or strategic.

Defining Residual Risk Vulnerability (Likelihood)

Residual risk vulnerability is the likelihood that a risk will occur in this area that prevents the achievement of objectives given current policies, procedures and controls, and prior experience/historical issues. High likelihood indicates a risk in this area has previously occurred, remediation did not take place, or a risk is almost certain to be realized again. Medium likelihood indicates that process and systems are/have been changing and controls have not had time to demonstrate effectiveness, or a risk in this area may be changing rapidly and controls may not be responding fast enough to prevent an issue. Controls to mitigate risk in this area are present but may not be formalized and therefore may not be consistently or effectively performed. Low likelihood indicates that the risk may occur only in rare circumstances. It could happen but probably never will.

Defining Impact

Impact is the severity of the effect on meeting the objective for this process and negative consequence. High impact indicates objectives will not be met resulting in a significant financial impact (>$ material to the company) that is not covered by insurance and includes fines and penalties, customer reimbursements, and inability to bill for or receive revenue. Severe operational impacts could include loss of life or injuries, critical systems being unavailable for more than X days when needed, a breach that results in loss of government information or critical intellectual property, or an inability to meet contractual deliverables. Compliance impact could include external regulatory action such as debarment, disqualified business systems, credit downgrade, or other actions that significantly alter the ability to operate. Medium impact indicates a moderate financial impact ($ range based on risk appetite) to the company, operational disruption that lasts less than X days, and compliance issues that result in regulatory corrective action short of systems disqualification. Low impact indicates minimal financial impact (<$ a specified based on risk appetite) and negligible operational/systems disruption (intermittent or less than an hour), while objectives will still be met.

Overall Risk Rating

The overall risk rating considers both the residual risk vulnerability and the impact, with a heavier weighting toward impact. For instance, if the residual risk vulnerability is low and the impact is high, the overall risk rating is medium.

Risk Monitoring

We can also add value by monitoring for regulatory changes and risk events that other companies are experiencing. There are numerous free or inexpensive services that offer risk insights. Most of the large accounting firms have newsletters that discuss risks. The Institute of Internal Auditors has some excellent monthly publications, such as Emerging News from the Audit Executive Center. One of the simplest ways to stay current is to leverage Google Alerts at GoogleAlerts. com. Type in a key word or phrase and Google will send a daily summary of any internet articles or mentions related to the topic chosen. For instance, if you work in banking and want to keep informed of the Dodd–Frank Act, set up an alert for "Dodd–Frank." The events of the day, related to the topic, can then be forwarded to your customer as a value-added piece of information. Of course, we need to be judicious in determining whether the information is relevant before sharing with the customer. I've received many notes of appreciation for proactively sharing information in this manner. It's an example of how we can connect with our customer outside of an audit engagement. It builds mutual trust and commitment. Sometimes our customers with second line of defense responsibilities are overwhelmed with other priorities to actively monitor changing risks. There have been instances where my customers were unaware of a new regulation until I shared it via a Google Alerts notification. Customers will start to think of internal audit differently when we proactively help them achieve objectives.

Employee Risk Surveys

Sending a risk survey to all employees at the company is a great way of assessing the tone at the middle and identifying risk perceptions from the bottom-up. The information creates ah-ha moments for management and the executive team about what individual contributors consider to be the most pressing risks facing the enterprise. There are many good survey tools available to support the assessment. Sending separate surveys by division creates a distinct risk profile for each business leader to review. Keep the surveys short to encourage greater participation.

The importance of a good tone at the top is well understood. How the CEO and executive team behave sends clear signals to the rest of the organization. Sometimes tone is lost or diluted as it moves further down the chain of command to middle management. Therefore, it's important to also assess tone at the middle or said another way, the tone provided my middle management supervisors and managers. Ask employees to rate their level of agreement with each of the following six statements with a rating scale of "strongly agree," "agree," "neither agree nor disagree," "disagree," or "strongly disagree."

- I have the knowledge and training to meet compliance requirements associated with my job.
- I am encouraged to ensure that financial records are accurate and truthful, regardless of the financial impact.
- I am encouraged to follow policies by my manager.
- My manager consistently demonstrates high standards of ethical conduct.

- If I reported a violation of the Standards of Conduct and Ethics to my manager, I believe appropriate action would be taken.
- I know what action to take if I become aware of unethical or fraudulent behavior.

The second part of the survey can ask employees to "tell us in a few words, what you believe to be the single most significant risk facing the company." The results can be shared with the executive team, and the detailed comments for each division shared with the respective division president. Internal audit can leverage the survey data to support audit planning. The results can also be shared with the Ethics Officer.

Surveys provide a direct, unfettered view of what employees are thinking and may identify areas of concern that should be addressed through focused training with the Ethics Officer or even warrant addition of an audit or special project to the audit plan. Following up with concerns reported is critical to making certain the employee that responded feels heard. Ensure that identification of the individual that responded is not shared with management. However, it is understood that the survey responses are not anonymous, and internal audit has the ability to follow up with concerns.

Risk Workshops

Facilitating risk workshops can add value for risk owners as they contemplate changes to processes, entering new lines of business, or if there are other changes in the business environment that need assessment. Start with the objectives for the business unit/function. In conjunction with a selection of knowledgeable representatives, brainstorm risks that could prevent objectives from being met. Rate those risks based on inherent likelihood and impact. Determine whether existing policies, procedures, and controls mitigate the likelihood of the risk occurring. Next assess the residual likelihood, given those policies, procedures, and controls identified. If there are no policies, procedures, or controls that address the likelihood of the risk, evaluate management options for addressing the risk. Typical options include avoidance, acceptance, exploit, mitigation, and transfer. Avoidance indicates elimination of the cause of the risk as possible. Putting a plan in place to make sure the risk in this area can never happen. Acceptance indicates that the risk is deemed reasonable by management given current controls and no additional immediate action is necessary. A contingency plan may be implemented to address the risk if it occurs. Exploit indicates leveraging the risk to realize business opportunities—the upside of a risk. Mitigate indicates that an action will be planned to make the risk less of a problem if it occurs. Transfer indicates sharing the risk with a third party, thereby reducing the exposure for the company—an example of this would be insurance or outsourcing. Facilitating risk workshops provide the management team with more information and options as they make business decisions. Results from the risk workshops can be used to update the Functional Risk Landscape.

Division Risk Landscapes

Partnering with division business leadership—the various sectors or divisions within a company—to develop Division Risk Landscapes can add real value. Division Risk Landscapes can capture a summary profile of the division (locations, staffing, turnover), compliance statistics, top risks for the division, higher risk initiatives, and major customers. The purpose is to facilitate risk discussions with the division presidents and determine whether internal audit engagement is needed. The landscapes can be shared with the CFO and CEO.

Connecting the Dots

Perhaps the best way to add value is by connecting the dots about risks relationships and facilitating dialog among customers. The dialog can be both formal and informal. Send customers emails about risk interdependencies to help bridge the divide in understanding and resolving an unmitigated risk. When new risks or a change in a risk occurs, explore how it impacts the company beyond the immediate risk owner. Asking who else is affected by this risk can be powerful and eye-opening.

Schedule a monthly or quarterly meeting of functional risk owners to discuss current and emerging risks and concerns. Stakeholders share information on emerging regulations, changes in the risk environment, and challenges achieving objectives. Internal audit acts as the facilitator. It's amazing to observe the rich, useful discussions that

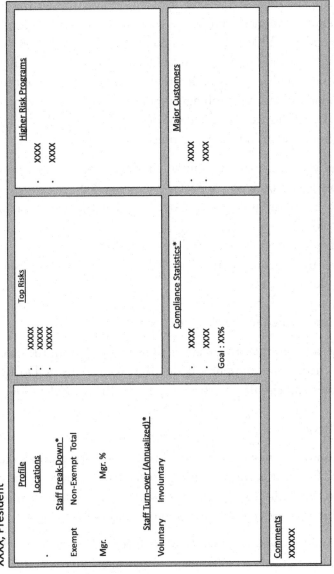

XXXX Division
XXXX, President

Profile

Locations

Staff Break-Down*
Exempt   Non-Exempt Total

Mgr.   Mgr. %

Staff Turn-over (Annualized)*
Voluntary Involuntary

Top Risks
. XXXXX
. XXXXX
. XXXXX

Higher Risk Programs
. XXXX
. XXXX

Compliance Statistics*
. XXXX
. XXXX
Goal : XX%

Major Customers
. XXXX
. XXXX

Comments
xxxxxx

Exhibit 4.6 Business risk landscape template.

* = as of December 21, 2018.

emerge by bringing people together to discuss their initiatives and the risks they are trying to overcome. People that may otherwise not ask for help, engage and have a reason to bridge knowledge gaps. When I facilitate these meetings, we start with a dedicated topic, for instance, a new company process and how it relates to everyone in the room. We then hold a Round Robin discussion, where each participant provides an update. What participants don't always appreciate is that by discussing projects, initiatives, and organizational changes, they are also talking about risk. A good internal audit facilitator helps the discussion along by asking probing questions. Voilà! Now everyone is interested, and they've connected the dots to their own functions and success. Some key facilitation questions to consider asking:

- Has anyone else faced a similar circumstance?
- How would/does "X" impact the organization?
- Are there any unknowns about "X" that the group should consider?
- What are other companies doing to address "X"?
- Does the function or organization have the resources necessary to address the risk?
- Does the risk rise to the level of concern that it should be communicated to the executive team?

Decide as a group if there are any actions required from the meeting or if risks need to be communicated to the executive team. Document the minutes and circulate to the group for further consideration.

Chapter Recap

Internal audit is a risk expert that adds value for the executive team, the Audit Committee, and functional owners by connecting the dots. Every internal audit team member is a sensor able to capture information within the risk environment. Internal audit adds value by

- Partnering with management to identify top risks to the company and how they relate to management's overall risk appetite. Helping management to develop top risk descriptions including interdependencies that could amplify the size of the risk or that require a coordinated response with other entities. Identifying risk influencers that affect velocity. Understanding near-term issues associated with the top risk that may require immediate attention. Assisting management in understanding all of its initiatives that support the risk response. Identifying ways that internal audit can engage with management through the audit plan or special projects to evaluate the sufficiency of the risk response given management's risk appetite.

- Facilitating the development of risk mitigation plans. Advising management on the design of controls that address the risk. Identifying the potential likelihood, velocity, and impacts of the risk. Helping management identify appropriate risk and control owners for accountability.
- Collaborating with process owners to identify risks to their meeting objectives.
- Creating a company-wide risk dashboard that captures major risks by mega process and function. Updating the risk dashboard as risk levels change. Identifying all associated risk owners.
- Developing division risk landscapes to assist leadership in understanding their risks.
- Facilitating a quarterly forum with all of the company's risk owners to discuss current and emerging risks. Identify ways risk owners can help each other.
- Developing a bottom-up risk assessment by sending a survey to all employees about their top risk concern and comparing it to the top risks identified by management. Following up on reported concerns and considering whether an audit plan response is necessary.
- Updating the audit plan to reflect changing risks.
- Alerting the management team when new risks emerge or existing risk levels change and require a response.

Notes

1 *New York Times*, Woman Killed by Electric Shock on Street, January 17, 2004.
2 *New York Times*, Utility Will Pay $7.2 Million in Electrocution, November 24, 2004.
3 US Customs and Immigration Enforcement, www.ice.gov/news/releases/consolidated-edison-employees-and-private-contractors-sentenced-bribery-scheme.

4 www.governor.ny.gov/news/governor-cuomo-announces-1533-million-settlement-con-edison-benefit-residential-and-commercial.
5 State of NY Public Service Commission, Case 09-M-0114.
6 ConEdison Company.
7 Institute of Internal Auditors, Standards for the Practice of Internal Auditing, January 1, 2017, https://na.theiia.org/standards-guidance/mandatory-guidance/pages/standards.aspx.
8 The Committee of Sponsoring Organization of the Treadway Commission, Enterprise Risk Management Framework.
9 The Committee of Sponsoring Organization of the Treadway Commission, Enterprise Risk Management—Understanding and Communicating Risk Appetites, www.coso.org/Documents/ERM-Understanding-and-Communicating-Risk-Appetite.pdf.

Bibliography

The Committee of Sponsoring Organization of the Treadway Commission, Enterprise Risk Management Framework.
Institute of Internal Auditors, Audit Executive Center: Member Survey--Adding Value.
https://cars.usnews.com/cars-trucks/best-cars-blog/2016/10/how-badly-has-the-vw-scandal-hurt-vw.
http://fortune.com/2018/08/01/chipotle-ecoli-food-safety-scare-ohio/.
https://money.cnn.com/2016/02/02/investing/chipotle-earnings-e-coli/index.html.
www.healthline.com/health/worst-foodborne-illness-outbreaks#eme-coliem.
www.reuters.com/article/us-volkswagen-emissions-dieselgate/vw-fined-one-billion-euros-by-german-prosecutors-over-emissions-cheating-idUSKBN1J92AI.
www.reuters.com/article/us-volkswagen-emissions-idUSKBN1E01W1.
www.reuters.com/article/us-volkswagen-emissions-suit/german-consumer-group-files-class-action-suit-on-behalf-of-volkswagen-owners-idUSKCN1N64OI.
www.usatoday.com/story/money/2018/06/27/chipotle-close-55-65-stores-year/740245002/.
www.wired.com/2016/01/chipotles-health-crisis-shows-fresh-food-comes-at-a-price/.

FACTOR 5

CHANGE MANAGEMENT AND PROCESS OPTIMIZATION

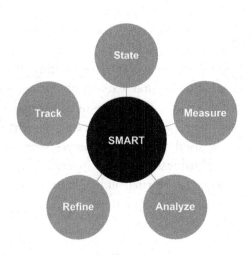

In 1987, Motorola Corporation was struggling with consistently producing high-quality products. A team of engineers sat down to understand why defects were occurring. They observed a lack of standards in production processes. To solve the problem, they created the Six Sigma System, which relied on data to minimize defects. Many other companies have adopted variations on Six Sigma since. The common theme is producing a consistent and high-quality product or service, while optimizing cost and efficiency. The basic concepts and tools of Six Sigma are universal and have been used throughout business for decades. Indeed, Raytheon Company has been a leader in using these principles throughout the enterprise to improve profitability and innovate new, high-value offerings for its customers.

We have a unique opportunity to positively impact the enterprise by facilitating change and helping customers optimize their processes, resulting in cost savings, revenue recoveries, and improved control efficiency and effectiveness. In other words—adding value. Internal auditors are uniquely qualified to deliver this value. We are process and facilitation experts with vast access to internal and external information including leading practices within industry.

Do you have a systematic method for helping customers improve their processes? Does the audit team include value-added deliverables for every engagement? The SMART system provides a method and tools to help customers solve important problems, improve their processes, and add value. Internal auditors are inherently problem solvers. Six Sigma tools and concepts are a natural fit for helping customers improve processes, optimize controls, and reduce costs. The SMART system outlined in this chapter uses these concepts and addresses how to solve important customer problems in the context of internal auditing. The SMART system raises the value of audits and assessments for our customers. It is intended to be used as a guide. Take pieces of each step in the system and apply them as appropriate for your business environment.

SMART can be used to help customers overcome significant obstacles to meeting business objectives (operational, financial, compliance, strategic). Use it for formal audits, management requests, and consulting engagements. It is a methodic approach to assess a business, function, or process problem.

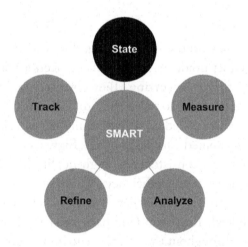

State (the Problem)

The first step is to State the Problem concisely and explain negative impacts of not having it resolved. The problem statement should include measurable data to support the business case for change. Focus on process, not people. Avoid initial judgments and explanations for the cause. Align the statement with the customer's goals and strategy.

As part of the statement, we need to build a business case or the value proposition for why the problem should be resolved. In the case of a formal audit, the business case was likely determined through the risk assessment process or a management request. The audit was deemed high risk, and therefore, it was added to the audit plan. During planning, the audit team should explore more details about why the audit was scheduled and understand what risks are being resolved. Estimate the value of doing the audit. What are the potential benefits and costs? What is the Audit Value Factor (AVF)? Remember from the Introduction:

$$Value Factor = Perceived Benefits / Perceived Costs$$

If the AVF is less than 1.0, reassess whether it is appropriate to invest internal audit resources.

For management requests and consulting engagements, we need to ask the question, why should we do this project? As part of the analysis, estimate the potential benefit vs. cost of taking on the effort as outlined in the introduction. Determine whether there is executive support or if the request is supported, for instance, by middle management only. Without executive support, it may be difficult to apply resources to resolve the problem during the improvement phase.

Determine the time period for resolving the problem. Projects that extend beyond 12 weeks may encounter changing business circumstances. There may be changes to processes, systems, and people that impact the initial problem statement. Resolution of the problem may be less meaningful to the customer if it takes too long. Generally, speed of delivery is considered a value-added benefit.

We have all witnessed an annual audit plan, developed in December with an audit scheduled for September, the following year, which is no longer relevant. So, imagine starting a project that lasts nine months. Surely the business environment and the customer's needs change in that time. We may be solving a problem that no longer exists or has changed, and the benefit may no longer endure. The business environment is dynamic, and we need to be responsive to customer needs and act quickly in completing projects.

Completing projects timely requires a firm commitment from the customer to be available, as part of the team, to finish the project on schedule. That's why it's critical to have a clear and agreed upon problem statement at the start including agreements on time and resource commitments.

Determine the resources required to support resolution of the problem. Consider the following:

- Which customers will be engaged?
- Who is the process owner?
- Who is the "customer of the customer" (who is impacted by the function or process being evaluated)?

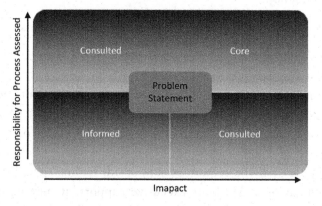

Exhibit 5.1   Customer identification quadrant.

The Core Customer is directly responsible for the problem being assessed and achieving the goals and objectives. The Consulted Customer has some responsibility for the process assessed or is impacted by services offered. The Informed Customer has no direct responsibility for the process or is minimally impacted by the services offered. There is a long list of well-intended projects with clear problem statements that failed because relevant customers were not engaged. The customer identification process continues through the Measure step, where the current state is assessed.

Consider a situation where a problem statement has been formed, the internal audit team spends hundreds of hours to identify the cause of the problem and makes recommendations for improvement, only to discover that a key customer who is a recipient of the changed process has not been considered. Time is wasted, the core customer is frustrated, the proposed improvement doesn't work, and value is not only not delivered but lost. All relevant customers should be identified and engaged as early as possible.

Utility connection example, customers include:

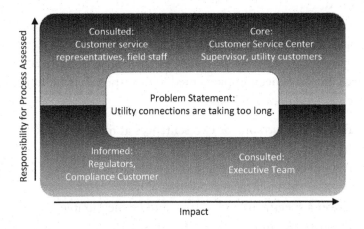

Exhibit 5.2   Example customer identification quadrant.

Determine how each customer wants to engage on the project. This instills trust and transparency in the assessment.

Determine the data necessary to support the problem statement.

- What data are necessary for the process to work?
- What are the sources of internal and external data?
- What data are produced by the function/process?

Determine what external information is useful in assessing the problem, such as benchmarks against peer or industry performance for the process being evaluated. Internal audit adds value by providing new information.

Are external parties, such as consultants, necessary to support the project from a subject-matter expertise perspective? Internal audit may not always have expertise or keep knowledge on the subject matter being evaluated. Co-source partners can supplement team knowledge.

Here is an example problem statement:

Utility customer connections are taking 5 days on average, resulting in unhappy customers and lost revenue.

Create a Vision Statement

Work with the customer to ensure executive support for the project. Ask executives to collaborate on the stated problem. Once the problem statement has been drafted, a vision for the future state should be developed.

Clearly state the vision for the project. A vision statement is a compelling vision of what the future state would look like if goals are accomplished. Look into the future imagining the improvements are in place and have been implemented for a sustained amount of time.

The vision statement should

- Be concise with one or two sentences at most
- Include the AVF based on data
- Avoid outlining the solution
- Be forward-looking and positive
- Cover a specific period of time and be measurable
- Describe the impact to the business
- Describe the gap between the current and future state in neutral terms

Here is an example of a vision statement.

Customers are safely connected to power within two business days, resulting in efficiencies throughout the process of $500,000 annually with an AVF of 10. The efficiencies will free up 10,000 hours of staff time to more productively connect customers.

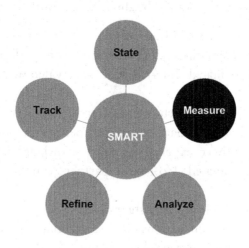

Measure

The first step in assessing the problem is to document the current state of the process. As discussed in the State step, all Inputs, Workflows, and Outputs should be understood. An Input is any information, resource, equipment, or people that contribute to the process being performed. A Workflow is how the process is actually performed using the inputs identified. An Output is anything that is delivered as a result of the Workflow.

Workflows

The simplest way to understand the current state is to document the process in a workflow map. A workflow map documents step by step how a process works. It's helpful in calling out inefficiencies such as duplicative efforts, rework, and delays, which can be further analyzed later.

Developing workflows is best done by including representatives of all stakeholders (customers) involved in the process documented. Invite the stakeholders to a collaboration session in an open space with white boards or walls conducive to laying out the process.

A designated member of the internal audit team leads the discussion. Establish ground rules for a facilitated discussion:

- Communicate the objectives of the collaboration ahead of time, so participants can prepare.
- Respect the process and participant inputs.
- Solicit expectations from participants before beginning.
- Outline expected outputs from the collaboration (process workflow).
- Create a "parking lot" for unrelated discussions. It's not unusual for a group discussing a process to get side tracked on unrelated discussions. If this occurs, note the topic on a list (parking lot) to be discussed in a separate venue.

Using sticky notes or a whiteboard, write down each major step in the process including actions, decision points, and data inputs and outputs. Sticky notes are useful to drive succinctness. If the action can't be summarized on one sticky note, it's likely more than one step/action and/or may require a side workflow of its own. While it may seem less efficient than directly documenting in an electronic flowchart, participants are more apt to be engaged if they are physically able to write down the steps themselves and move the sticky notes around the wall.

After the collaboration session, create an electronic version of the workflow. Software such as Visio and PowerPoint are useful tools. Use the following standard symbols:

Start/termination of the process.

Process step/action. The process step/action should identify the action owner and action taken in a brief statement.

Decision point. The decision point leads to a yes/no decision. This could be approving or rejecting a prior step's action or accepting or rejecting a submission.

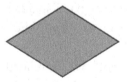

Data. It represents information that is received or produced as part of the workflow.

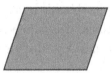

Connector. A connector represents the connection or continuation of a step to different workflow or continuation of the current workflow to another page.

Connection lines. They display the direction of the workflow.

Workflows can be a continuous stream or multilane (swim lane) displays. A continuous lane documents the process in sequential order, highlighting hand-offs in the activity boxes with return loops for decision outcomes as necessary. A swim lane workflow separates individual workflow steps by responsible action owner. Actions and decisions in a swim lane workflow move between stakeholder swim lanes to show how the action owners interact.

In our utility connection workflow example, the workflow follows:

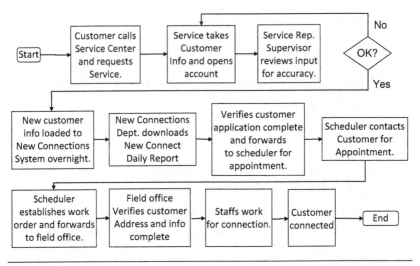

Exhibit 5.3 Example workflow.

Gemba

Once the process has been documented, it can be helpful to gather additional data to support the workflow. One technique is the classic Gemba approach. Gemba is a Japanese term meaning "the real thing." In the context of workflows, this means going to see how the process actually works. For example, going and observing each person's activity involved in the Utility Customer Connection Process. While observing the process:

- Record the amount of time it takes to complete a step in the workflow documented. Use time increments deemed appropriate for the workflow being assessed; generally, one min is suitable.
- Document the process performance. Does the process operate smoothly? What challenges were encountered?
- Observe whether systems and supporting tools worked effectively.
- Note any actions that seem overly complex. Does the action owner need to work around obstacles? Do the actions require referencing guidance or procedures or are they intuitive? Does Joe in Human Resources need to reformat extracts of information from systems to complete an action?
- Identify any excess movement of people or resources. Does Jane in Accounting need to physically walk over to another department to get information to support completion of an action?

Take the observations from Gemba and update the workflow. Send an electronic updated version of the workflow to the stakeholders involved in the process.

Examine the workflow, and identify any points of inefficiency. Consider

- Decision points that lead to work being re-performed
- Steps with multiple hand-offs
- Actions that require data from multiple systems
- Steps that require stakeholder work-arounds due to insufficient information or complexity in the current state of the process

Value-Add Analysis

While identifying points of inefficiency, assess the value of each step. This supports identification of wasted resources for reduction and elimination, leans out the process, supports customer success, facilitates cross-stakeholder knowledge exchange, and can result in cost savings and revenue recoveries.

Value-added actions meet three criteria: they are performed correctly the first time, they are additive to the process (new or transformed information or product), and they are considered valuable to the customer (benefits exceed cost of the action's completion). Value-added steps include

- Launching a new service, product, or application
- A changed service or product
- New features
- Improved service or quality
- Quicker delivery or improved convenience
- Improved compliance
- Refactoring computer code to increase efficiency

Actions that don't meet the value-added criteria are non-value added. Non-value-added steps fall into two categories—planned and unplanned non-value added. Planned non-value-added (planned waste) steps consist of activities that do not add value or support customer requirements but may be required to operate the business. Non-value-added planned steps may include

- Preparing administrative reports for another stakeholder's use
- Computer/peer code reviews
- Training
- Responding to customer questions or complaints
- Reviewing and approving reports
- Preparation time
- Inspections
- Meetings

Unplanned non-value-added steps (waste) consist of activities that do not add value or support customer requirements and are in effect a wasteful use of resources. Non-value-added unplanned steps may include

- Correction of errors or mistakes. Coding and data entry errors. Production mistakes.
- Overproduction of information or product. Designing features that customers don't want.
- Unnecessary movement of information or materials.
- Excess motion. Performing unnecessary analysis, testing, etc.
- Waiting time for inputs and outputs.
- Excess inventory. Excess information or physical inventory. Data are produced that are never used. The classic "TPS Report" from the movie Office Space.
- Unnecessary reviews and approvals.

Taking the value-add, non-value add analysis into consideration, we can now update our process map to identify value-added activities, waste, and planned waste.

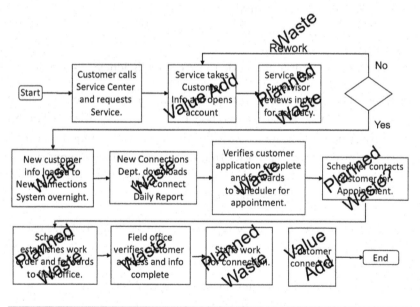

Exhibit 5.4   Example value-add analysis using workflow.

Going back to the Gemba data collected, reexamine the amount of time associated with each step to complete the action. Evaluate the amount of time elapsed between steps. This accounts for wait time-associated inputs or production of outputs; Joe may not be able to complete his action until he receives data from Jane. Identify "dead time" associated with each step. Dead time is the time between completion of the prior step and commencement of the next step. Dead time can be driven by resource constraints, such as action owners with competing priorities; Joe completed his action but was then distracted by another responsibility and didn't provide Jane with the information to start her action.

For our utility connection example, the Value-Add Analysis follows:

Step	Description	Responsible Person	Elapsed Time	Actual Time (minutes)	Dead Time	Value Add	Non-Value Add
1	Customer calls Service Center and requests service.	Customer, Call Center	0	0	0	0	0
2	Service takes Customer info and opens account	Call Center Rep	0	20	1	20	0
3	Service Rep. Supervisor reviews input for accuracy.	Supervisor	21	20	40	0	20
4	Rework	Call Center Rep	60	90	40	0	90
5	New customer info loaded to New Connections System overnight.	Supervisor	130	30	480	0	30
6	New Connections Dept. downloads New Connect Daily Report	New Connects	510	30	60	0	30
7	Verifies customer application complete and forwards to scheduler for appointment.	New Connects	90	60	60	0	60
8	Scheduler contacts Customer for Appointment.	Scheduler	120	20	20	20	0
9	Scheduler establishes work order and forwards to field office.	Scheduler	40	60	120	0	60
10	Field office verifies customer address and infocomplete	Field Office	180	60	2880	0	60
11	Staffs work for connection.	Field Office	2940	120	1440	0	120
12	Customer connected	Field Office	1560	60	120	60	0
	Total				5261	100	470

Exhibit 5.5   Value-Add Analysis chart.

For each non-value-added planned and unplanned step, estimate the cost of the activities. Use an average hourly rate for stakeholder time in the process. For instance, if Joe's hourly rate is $50 and he spent 10 hours on non-value-added unplanned activities, resulting in $500 in potential savings. The workflow cycle is one month, so the company could save up to $6,000 by eliminating the non-value-added activities associated with his responsibilities.

The Value-Add Analysis is optional depending on the problem that is being evaluated. It can be worthwhile if a workflow is already being developed. The incremental effort is minimal, yet can identify significant potential cost savings from inefficiencies.

Desirable and Undesirable Effects

The next phase of the workflow assessment is looking at Desirable Effects (DEs) and Undesirable Effects (UDEs) in the process. A DE is anything that positively impacts the performance of the process, supports customer achievement of objectives, or leads to customer value. A UDE, also known as a "pain point", is anything that negatively impacts performance of the process, prevents the customer from meeting objectives, or leads to customer dissatisfaction or non-value.

Reconvene the stakeholder team originally utilized to document the current state workflow. Take a few moments and walk-through the updated workflow to re-familiarize the group with the overall process and main steps.

Remind the team about the overall problem statement that is being addressed. Using sticky notes again, ask participants to individually brainstorm, without discussion, what the DEs and UDEs are in the process:

- Ask them to write one DE or UDE per sticky note.
- The DE or UDE should be self-explanatory.
- Avoid assigning a cause.
- Avoid including a solution to UDEs.

Have participants place the sticky notes on the wall. The collaboration team now groups the sticky notes according to themes. This provides participants with insights from colleagues. Review the major categories of themes and encourage discussion. This will spur additional ideas about what is and isn't working in the current process and may lead to additional DEs and UDEs or themes. For team members working remotely, consider using software, such as Mural.

Keep note of DEs. The customer will want these to remain, and any changes to the process should avoid negatively impacting the current DEs in the process workflow.

Team Prioritization of UDEs for Analysis

The collaboration team now prioritizes the UDEs to be addressed as part of the audit/project. Use dot stickers or voting software, such as Poll Everywhere for the exercise. Each team member gets a set number of votes, which will depend on the number of themes identified. A good rule of thumb for voting: less than ten themes (three votes), 10–15 themes (six votes), 15–20 themes (nine votes). Each team member then votes on the topic that they think has the most impact or is most important to resolve. Team members can weight votes toward one or more topics. For instance, if someone thinks UDE #1 is most important, they could hypothetically, use all of their votes to prioritize that topic. The topics with the highest vote totals are prioritized for analysis.

Validation

Review the UDEs for correlation with the overall problem statement. Consider de-prioritizing or setting aside UDEs that are unrelated for later analysis. Meet with the core customers and executive sponsors to validate the proposed UDE's for analysis.

Analyze

The analyze phase is used to assess the UDEs noted in the Measure phase and identify root causes for resolution. The root cause/s identified should be supported by data. Refer to the Data Analytics Factor for more information on data analytic techniques. The focus throughout the analysis is verifying that the root cause/s identified address the original problem statement. Would the root causes identified fix the problem that is trying to be resolved?

For each UDE, determine whether data are available to support the analysis. Data from the original Value-Add Analysis should be leveraged. Collect additional data through interviews with process owners and surveys and via data analytics as necessary.

Surveys

Surveys are an effective means of gathering additional data on a process and customer satisfaction. There are whole guides dedicated to the art of surveying. It's an opportunity to gain perspective quickly from a broader group of people. Surveys are most effective when concise and simple. Using predefined answers will quicken results analysis. There are many good online survey tools available.

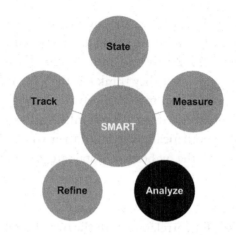

Before sending a survey, work with the customer to develop the questions and overall tone. Depending on the objective of the survey, it's important not to bias survey participants by asking leading questions or asking questions with a positive or negative predisposition. If the survey is expressly to solicit feedback on problems in a process or how a process can be improved, then avoiding bias is less important. Include a brief introduction describing the purpose of the survey, the amount of time required to complete it, whether the responses will be anonymous, and when the survey will close.

Root Cause Analysis

The objective of a root cause analysis is to identify the underlying, actionable cause for the problem statement and UDEs in the process. There are several techniques for doing a root cause analysis including five whys, Ishikawa (fishbone) cause and effect analysis, and Cause and Effect Matrix. We will review each method.

Five Whys

Start with the UDE/s noted in the Measure step. Each major UDE is analyzed for its root cause. Ask the question: why did the UDE occur? That leads to a Direct Cause. Ask again, why did the Direct Cause occur? That will lead to one or more Contributing Causes. Ask again, why did the Contributing Cause occur? That will lead to one or more additional Contributing Causes. Continue to ask "why" until the causes are no longer actionable.

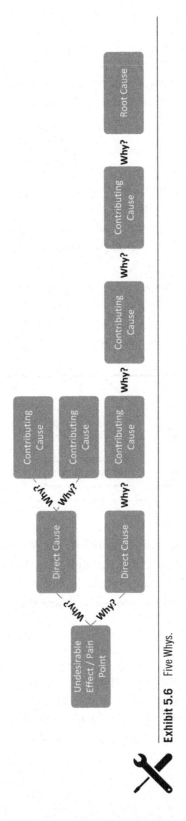

Exhibit 5.6   Five Whys.

The Ishikawa diagram was created by Kaoru Ishikawa in 1968 to improve the quality of management processes. It is also known as a Cause and Effect or Fishbone Diagram because of its shape. Each UDE gets its own Cause and Effect Analysis and is analyzed for root cause related to five major factors:

- *People*: anyone involved in the process
- *Methods*: how the process is performed and supporting elements such as policies and procedures
- *Machines*: equipment, systems, etc. to support the process
- *Materials*: tools, materials, etc. used to support the process
- *Measurements*: key performance indicators and data generated from the process to signal performance

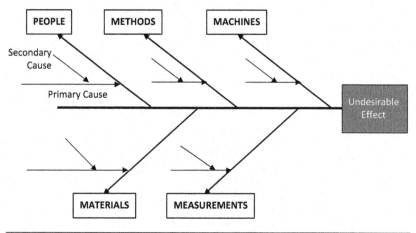

Exhibit 5.7   Ishikawa diagram.

The Ishikawa diagram is useful if the team is having difficulty brainstorming the root cause through Five Whys or needs a more structured approach to causal analysis. It forces consideration for the major sources of inputs to a process and how they contribute to UDEs.

Synthesize Causes

Sort through and prioritize the root causes identified. Some root causes may not be addressed due to a lack of resources, control over decision-making, or because they don't resolve enough UDEs to make an investment worthwhile. Using a spreadsheet, take each of the root causes identified and list them in a spreadsheet column on separate lines. Document each of the UDEs noted during the Measure step in a row separated by columns.

Exhibit 5.8   UDEs Prioritization Matrix

	UDE	UDE	UDE	UDE	UDE	UDE	UDE	UDE	UDE	TOTAL
Root cause #1	X	X	X	X		X		X		6
Root cause #2	X		X		X		X			4
Root cause #3		X				X			X	3
Root cause #4		X								1

Since resources are finite, root causes with the biggest impact should be prioritized for resolution. At this point, we also consider the value of resolving each of the UDEs. Going back to the Value Factor, calculate the estimated Value Factor for each root cause and UDE combination.

$$\text{Value Factor} = \text{Perceived Benefits of Resolving UDE} /$$
$$\text{Perceived Cost of Resolving Root Cause}$$

Monetize the perceived benefits and costs of addressing the root cause. Refer back to the Value-Add Analysis exercise for a complete list of potential non-value-added activities.

Examples of potential (perceived) benefits may include

- Reductions in rework. Calculate the amount of rework time eliminated using an average hourly rate for personnel involved in the process. For instance, if resolving the root cause reduces rework by 100 hour/month at an average of $100/hour, the total benefit is $10,000 a month or $120,000 annually.
- Reductions in administrative time due to excess handling of data. Here again, the reduction in administrative time can be calculated by the number of hours involved and the hourly rate.
- Elimination or reduction in unnecessary reviews and approvals.
- Improved revenue or profit. If resolving the root cause will positively impact revenue or profit, estimate the benefit. Improved profit or revenue may occur if customers have provided feedback that revenue was lost due to a poor experience interacting with company processes or people.
- Improved information processing time.
- Added features or benefits to the product or process.

Document the perceived benefits and costs for each root cause. This detail can be used later to build the business case for making a change and designing solutions. Using the same spreadsheet, update the boxes denoted with the AVFs calculated (below is hypothetical).

Exhibit 5.9 UDEs Prioritization Matrix Example

	UDE	UDE	UDE	UDE	UDE	UDE	UDE	UDE	UDE	TOTAL
Root cause	2	10	0.50	3		15		0.10		30.6
Root cause	50		11		0.25		4			65.25
Root cause		100				10.50			9	119.5
Root cause		0.50								0.50

Priorities can change when taking into consideration the AVF. What appeared to be clear case for root cause #1 before calculating the AVF, now appears less compelling. The AVF helped provide objectivity in prioritizing root causes for resolution. This is useful when we have audit observations and need to justify recommendations. Being able to explain the perceived or expected benefits vs. the cost of implementing a solution is compelling.

Two final questions should be asked:

1. Will resolution of the selected root causes solve the problem identified during the "State" step?
2. Are we able to meet the project customer's vision by addressing these root causes?

If the answer is no, the process should be further evaluated for additional root causes.

Refine

Now that the root causes have been selected, we need to support the customer in designing a solution. Internal auditors are sometimes hesitant to help design management action plans for fear of impacting objectivity and independence. The bottom line is that the customer is the ultimate owner and has the final decision on design. Avoiding design assistance can leave the customer feeling unaided at a crucial point in the process.

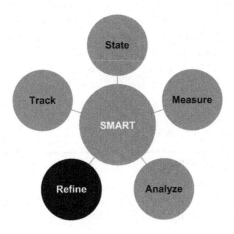

Solution design can be complex and create unintended negative consequences. We need to anticipate potential pitfalls. There are few system implementations, for instance, that don't result in unanticipated collateral damage. Information that was available before, now isn't. The same holds true for internal audit recommendations and management action plan designs.

Brainstorm Solutions

Too often, solutions and management action plans are designed in a vacuum with little information. We need to bring together the "core customers" and a selection of "consulted customers" to brainstorm potential solutions. By engaging consulted customers early, we collaboratively design the solution, which leads to quicker acceptance.

There are many instances of internal auditors making recommendations, which the auditee feels compelled to implement, without consideration for downstream impacts. There is also a reluctance among some internal auditors to consider all of the options to resolving a root cause. This is driven by lack of creativity, time constraints, and pressure to issue reports, poor customer relationships, and lack of subject-matter expertise.

As the facilitator of the brainstorming session, work to identify three alternative solutions and ask the participants the following:

- What are the obvious solutions to the root cause?
- What could be achieved quickly?
- What could be achieved with more time and resources?

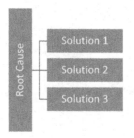

Exhibit 5.10   Solutions identification.

Consider the following additional factors:

- Does the solution negatively impact any of the existing DEs in the current process? If so, weigh the trade-off of the solution with negative consequences.
- Who would own the solution/management action plan?
- Has the solution owner been involved in design? If not, validate the solution with them.
- Is the solution owner empowered to implement the change? Are they able to muster the resources necessary to make the change?

Failure Mode and Effects Analysis

How often have internal audit recommendations and management action plans had unintended consequences? Failure Mode and Effects Analysis is a technique, originally created by the US military, to anticipate what could go wrong in a new product. The concept has since been extended for use in manufacturing, services, and by innovators.

The technique is useful for internal audit recommendations and management action plans to anticipate and control for potential negative consequences to the process. In essence, we are improving the solution and making the outcome more successful before implementation. This raises the overall value of recommendations. Failure Mode and Effects Analysis asks three basic questions:

- What could go wrong with the solution/management action plan? How will core and consulted customers and other stakeholders receive the change (positive or negative)? How might the solution/management action plan be undermined by those who don't agree?
- What is the impact if this occurred?
- How can the solution/management action plan be improved to control or prevent the negative impact?

First, we consider what the possible failures are of the solution. We brainstorm and identify these individually. Next, we assess the potential severity of the failure. The team can assign a rating (1–10) with 10 being most severe and 1 being inconsequential. The likelihood of the failure is assessed and again rated on a scale of 1–10 with 1 representing a highly unlikely occurrence and 10 representing a certain occurrence.

The two ratings (severity and likelihood) are multiplied to arrive at an overall risk of failure score. This is repeated for each potential failure of the proposed solution/management action plan. Lastly, we update the solution/management action plan to anticipate or correct for these potential failures. A template for this assessment follows:

FAILURE MODE AND EFFECTS ANALYSIS (FMEA)							
PROCESS_____	S = Severity of the effects of failure (1 = low, 10 = high) O = Probability of failure occurring (1 = low, 10 = high) D = Likelihood failure is detected (1 = low, 10 = high) RPN = Risk Priority Number (S x O)						
Proposed Management Action Plan	Potential Failure Mode	Potential Effects of Failure Mode	S	Potential Cause of Failure	O	RPN	Potential Modification to Action Plans to Minimize Failure and Negative Effects
What is the proposed management action plan or internal audit recommendation related to an observation / finding?	In what ways could this action plan not meet the intended requirements?	What collateral damage / negative impact could occur to the process, business, resources, or meeting objectives? What could go wrong?		What would cause the failure to occur?			What additional actions could improve the management action plan to minimize failure of the action plan, bad outcomes and negative consequences?

Exhibit 5.11   Failure Mode and Effects Analysis template.

The following is an example of a Failure Mode and Effects Analysis:

FAILURE MODE EFFECTS ANALYSIS (FMEA)							
PROCESS: INFORMATION SECURITY		S = Severity of the effects of failure (1 = low, 10 = high) O = Probability of failure occurring (1 = low, 10 = high D = Likelihood failure is detected (1 = low, 10 = high) RPN = Risk Priority Number (S x O)					
Proposed Management Action Plan	Potential Failure Mode	Potential Effects of Failure Mode	S	Potential Cause of Failure	O	RPN	Potential Modification to Action Plans to Minimize Failure and Negative Effects
Require all employees traveling out-of-country to use a loaner-laptop computer without company data.	• Computer is not properly configured or not configured for user needs. • User is unable to unlock computer. • Computer lacks destination connectivity / Wi-Fi capability. • Necessary software is not loaded to the computer. • Employee forgets multi-factor authentication card because they are using a loaner laptop bag. • User not provided power cord. • Laptop bags unavailable.	The employee arrives at their destination and is unable to conduct business. Corporate IT is unavailable because the destination location is 10 hours ahead of office hours. The employee is unable to deliver a critical presentation to the client.	10	• There is no loaner laptop preparation checklist. • Loaner laptops are not tested before distribution. • IT does not provide an overview of loaner laptop capabilities.	5	50	The IT organization will develop a comprehensive loaner laptop preparation checklist to include configurations that meet traveling staff needs, relevant software installations, and any necessary hardware and power supplies. IT will identify a person that will be on call to support the executive upon their arrival.

Exhibit 5.12   Failure Mode and Effects Analysis example.

Failure Mode and Effects Analysis is a valuable tool to improve success and minimize negative impacts when making any major change at a company.

Communicating the Solution/Management Action Plans

The good news is that we've included our core and consulted customers in the design of the solution/management action plans. We now need to consider other stakeholders downstream that may use the revised process. Communications with stakeholders should reflect what they need to hear. For some that may mean a simple email outlining the changes, for others it may mean a personal meeting with details about the change and how the team arrived to the solution. It's always best to apply the Platinum Rule: treat others as *they* wish to be treated. In other words, communicate the change to them in a way that best suits their needs.

Refinement of the Solution/Action Plans

Once the solution/management action plan has been implemented and some time has passed (generally within one month), we will want to solicit feedback on the change. This can be done through in person discussions, via email, or for feedback from a larger group, via electronic survey. Ask the following simple questions:

- Have you used X process since the change? If so, has the process improved from your perspective?
- If you feel the process has improved, please share your experience.
- If you feel the process has not improved, please share your experience.
- What additional changes would you suggest for the process?

By asking for feedback shortly after the change, we continue to build trust with the process users and demonstrate willingness to revisit the solution for further refinement and improvement.

Analyze the feedback and consider possible changes to the solution. If the solution is revised, re-perform the Failure Mode and Effects Analysis on the proposed changes to minimize secondary negative impacts from the revisions.

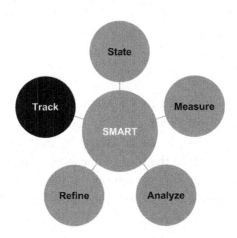

Track

The last step in the process is to track the progress of the changes made. Inherent in tracking is a need to have clearly identified action owners, as well as metrics. We also want to make sure that the change is institutionalized. This means updating policies and procedures, training programs, and finding additional champions to make sure the change takes hold.

Solution/Management Action Plan Owner

Having a clearly identified owner for the action plan who is responsible and accountable for its success is crucial. I prefer to emphasize the action owner's role vs. an individual's name. We've all probably experienced a situation where a person leaves a job, a project falls by the wayside, and change is halted. Then when a new person fills the role, the actions that the prior occupant committed to are disregarded. When we name a role as responsible for an action plan vs. an individual, it transcends staff change and stays tied to the role.

The action plan should have clear deliverable dates. If the solution is a phased implementation, outline milestone delivery dates with specific deliverables. Management action plan completion dates that are too far into the future risk becoming irrelevant since the process itself may change. Shorter implementation deadlines keep the core and consulted customers engaged, allow them to use the changed process and provide feedback, and enable iterative improvements sooner.

Metrics

Metrics on the revised process validate whether the management action plan is working or not. If the goal is to improve process efficiency, metrics should be designed to monitor that. Metrics should be linked back to the original problem statement and vision for the process, function, or subject of the assessment. Metrics should be quantitative when possible and use standardized units of measurements.

Validate Value

The final step of track is to validate whether anticipated value has been achieved. This is done once changes to the process have had time to take effect. The metrics developed are leveraged as part of the validation. Going back to the original calculation for the AVF, assess whether the perceived/expected benefits have been achieved.

A recap of potential benefits:

- Reductions in rework
- Reductions administrative time due to excess handling of data
- Elimination or reduction in unnecessary reviews and approvals
- Improved revenue or profit
- Improved information processing time
- Added features or benefits to the product or process

We can also calculate value from the original Value-Add Analysis in the Measure step. Identify those actions in the process that have either been eliminated or streamlined and calculate the time saved.

If the anticipated value has not been achieved, assess where the new process has fallen short. It could be the design is not working as intended or the original benefits were overstated. Design issues can be addressed through an additional iteration of solution improvement with further stakeholder feedback.

Solutions should never be stagnant, as circumstances evolve continuously. The SMART system is intended to be an iterative method of improving processes and solving problems.

Chapter Recap

Serially successful innovators have a method to support their achievements. Likewise, internal auditors need a system to help customers improve processes, identify cost savings and efficiencies, accelerate change, and design the best future state solutions. In other words, a method to consistently deliver value. The SMART system offers such a system. SMART raises the value of audits and special projects for our customers. Start by stating and understanding the problem to be addressed. Measure current practices and business workflows for understanding. Analyze the root causes of UDEs and pain points.

Prioritize resolving the most impactful root causes. Refine solutions to address the desired future state. Make certain to anticipate things that could go wrong and update designs to address potential failures. Track the solutions and validate whether the expected value has been delivered. If it hasn't, revisit the solution and iterate. Remember that solutions should be dynamic and responsive to new circumstances and conditions.

Bibliography

Dr. Curtis R. Carlson and William W. Wilmot, The Five Disciplines of Innovation, 2006, Crown Business.
https://en.wikipedia.org/wiki/Failure_mode_and_effects_analysis.
https://en.wikipedia.org/wiki/Kaoru_Ishikawa.
https://en.wikipedia.org/wiki/Six_Sigma.
www.qualitymag.com/articles/84187-motorola-a-tradition-of-quality.

FACTOR 6
DATA ANALYTICS

The emergence of Robotic Process Automation (RPA) is a hot topic. RPA is the use of software to perform tasks otherwise performed by humans, particularly tasks that are repetitive in nature. Think of it as a sophisticated Excel macro. Likewise, progress in augmented intelligence continues to complement human capabilities in analyzing and solving problems. These developments and others will drive the urgent need for internal audit to adapt its approach, understand how new technology can be leveraged to advance value, and provide deeper insights for customers. There is a more immediate need—the more effective use of analytics.

Internal auditors have been told for years about the importance of data analytics. Yet there are still departments performing limited analytics or doing so selectively with a subset of the team. In this chapter we'll outline why analytics is important and the opportunity to deliver value for customers through cost reductions and recoveries. Every operation, function, and process generate data, which are valuable potential insights to harvest. The only limit is your imagination!

We leverage software to perform data analytics, but in order to achieve value-added results, we need to understand which questions to ask, what relevant data to examine, and how the problem relates to the data. We need to decipher what is important and what is not. Data analytic software is only as effective as the person behind the design of the analysis. It's really about critical thinking skills.

Analytics enable audit teams to recommend transformative change. Customers often don't have the time or technical capability to understand their own data. Data empowers customers to make better decisions and optimize performance. It provides powerful value to the enterprise including insights on how to reduce the cost of operations, recover and optimize revenue, monitor compliance, lean out business processes, optimize information systems, and detect fraud.

We are able to eliminate random or haphazard sampling for testing by using data analysis. Instead, we can analyze 100% of transactions and focus on outliers for further examination.

Delivering Value in Opening Meetings

In formal audits, analytics should be performed during preplanning and planning to help prioritize the scope and add value for customers. How often do auditors hold an opening meeting with customers and walk through routine information about the objectives and scope, the audit process, confirmation of stakeholders, timing of the audit, and how the results will be communicated? Is this information important? Certainly. Would our customers consider it valuable? Unlikely. It's more perfunctory.

How many opening meetings tell the customer something they don't know? What if the opening meeting included profiles of the customer's data with insights and trends? I believe a meeting should not happen unless there is value derived for the customer. Providing customers with an "ah-ha" moment before an audit starts builds the team's credibility, gets the customer's attention, and focuses the project on value. Performing an analysis of customer data and sharing the results in the opening meeting spurs great conversations. Customers are focused on execution and often don't have the time to sit back and evaluate data patterns associated with their business.

Consider providing initial data analytics on the following in opening meetings:

- Profile of the customer's activity (transactions, processing time, revenue, expenditures, any other data associated with customer processes) over a select period of time
- Trend comparison vs. other company data, for instance revenue, full-time equivalents (FTEs), profit, etc.
- Cost trends per transaction
- Activity that has the most rework/rejections based on system time stamps

Critical Thinking and Planning

Data analysis is often thought of as a mechanical effort. Request a data extract, load the data into software, run a few predefined scripts, and review the results. Lost is the critical thinking required to achieve value-added results. The National Council for Excellence in Critical Thinking defines critical thinking as the "intellectually disciplined process of actively and skillfully conceptualizing, applying, analyzing, synthesizing, and/or evaluating information gathered from, or generated by, observation, experience, reflection, reasoning, or communication, as a guide to belief and action."

We need to conceptualize the possibilities for the operation being analyzed. Consider the following:

- Is there an important problem to solve? If so, what is the problem?
- What do we envision as the outcome for the analysis?
- What value will be provided? What are the perceived benefits?
- At the end of the analysis, what "ah-ha" moment are we looking to provide for the customer?
- Will the customer's fundamental thinking about their operation change?

Partner with the customer to identify his or her priorities for the analysis. Understand the operation before analyzing the associated data. Leverage documented workflows and other artifacts as discussed in the chapter on Process Optimization. Consider the following questions:

- How has the operation changed over the last 12, 24, and 36 months? Include all relevant data.
- What impact have changes had on the operation and the enterprise overall?
- What spending does the operation control? Follow the money.
- What drives operational expenditures? What could go wrong?
- How does the operation impact revenue?
- What types of information systems are used, and how do they relate to other operations within the company?
- Can data be manipulated?

Sources of Potential Cost Savings through Data Analytics

The following are areas where I have delivered significant cost savings to businesses through the use of data analytics. The unique circumstances of each company will determine savings. For instance, if a company has a dedicated team to continuously analyze and optimize spending, the category may already be optimized.

Travel and Expense

Travel and expense data analysis can typically identify cost savings of 3% of expenditures (e.g., 3% of $10,000,000 is $300,000). It is a long-standing area for potential fraud and abuse.

The first step is to identify all possible sources of data, which would normally include an extract from the travel and expense payment system, the external travel provider (agency used to book travel, if one used). The data extract should include employee name, employee identification, expense type (airfare, hotel, meal, transportation, incidental, etc.), vendor/service provider name, expense amount, expense date, travel purpose, travel dates, travel locations, and foreign exchange rates.

Expense Reasonableness   Assess the reasonableness of cost incurred in compliance with policy.

- Examine airfare class, taxi/limo services, airline club memberships, meals, and alcohol.

Hotel Expenditures   Hotel expenditures offer a variety of cost saving and recovery opportunities. Employees may stay at non-preferred hotels or non-preferred rates, resulting in excess cost. Hotel stays may not align with travel dates. Hotel packages may mask meals, such as breakfast, provided.

- Analyze air travel dates vs. hotel check-in and check-out dates. Identify and examine hotel check-out dates that are after return flights. This is a potential area for fraud, where an expense not actually incurred is being reimbursed.
- Analyze hotel expenditures vs. average hotel rates for each destination. Travel agencies maintain average nightly rate data, and it is normally available upon request.
- Identify nightly rates that significantly exceed average rates for further examination.

- Perform additional investigative work regarding the type of room reserved, and hotel package or additional amenities provided outside of company policy. For example, an employee may reserve an upgraded room (larger room, room with a view, spa room, etc.) or a suite instead of a standard room.

Airfare Booking Timeliness   Analyze airfare booking timeliness relative to travel dates. Airfare booked within seven days of travel typically brings a significant premium.

- Examine date of reservation vs. dates of travel, cost of fare, and fees.
- Calculate the number of days between reservation and travel dates.
- Stratify by difference in reservation and travel dates.
- Calculate median $ airfare price for each grouping.
- Calculate $ variance between groupings (<7 days before travel, 7–14 days before travel, and >21 days before travel) and median $ airfare in population.
- Calculate potential $ savings for flights booked <7 days before travel, versus the cost of booking those flights >21 days before travel. Travel agencies can provide average discounting available for booking further in advance.

Airfare Credits   Analysis of airfare credits. Unused airfare credits are generated by cancellations. It's not uncommon for companies, especially small to medium size businesses, to not identify and track unused credits. Employees may use the credits for personal use without company knowledge because they are associated with the employee's name. I have seen circumstances where hundreds of thousands of dollars of airline credits go unused because the company is not tracking credit balances and expiration dates.

- Obtain data extract of unused airfare credits from travel providers and airlines, employee names, airline, $ amount of credits, original travel dates, and credit expiration dates.
- Analyze credits by employee for patterns.
- Calculate difference between outstanding credits and change fees for net credits available.

- For employees with excess credits and/or high-volume rebooking activity, verify appropriate use of credits for business purposes.
- Identify airfare credit expirations according to original booking date and airline policy for use before expiration. Certain airlines will allow pooling of credits for use by other employees.

Duplicate Reimbursements   Employees may be reimbursed more than once for the same expense. Travel providers may double charge the company for services. Consider obtaining an extract of vendor payments for this analysis, depending on company system configuration and processes. Employees may be reimbursed through both the travel and expense process and the normal payment process.

- Analyze expense reimbursement amounts and dates for duplication across employee name and identification.
- Identify expense reimbursements with same amount to the same employee on the same date, for the same amount to different employees on same date, and for the same amount to different employees with different dates. Multiple employees may submit reimbursement requests for the same expenditure, resulting in duplicative reimbursement. Extract outlier activity for further analysis.

Surface Transportation Providers   Analyze taxi, limo, train, and other surface transportation reimbursements. Surface transportation is often paid by the traveler using cash. Taxi providers typically furnish blank receipts, which can be manipulated by the traveler.

- Analyze taxi reimbursements by employee using Benford's Law Analysis. Beneford's Law is the principle that in any large, randomly produced set of natural numbers, such as tables of logarithms or corporate sales statistics, around 30% will begin with the digit 1, 18% with 2, and so on, with the smallest percentage beginning with 9. The law is applied in analyzing the validity of statistics and financial records. Examine outliers for further testing.
- Analyze taxi reimbursement dates compared to hotel dates and airfare transportation dates. Examine taxi reimbursements for unexpected dates and locations (employee request

reimbursement for a taxi on date outside of the inbound and return flight dates).

- Analyze taxi reimbursements on the same day or for the same amount across the employee population. Multiple employees may request reimbursement for the same taxi fare. This is also covered under Duplicate Reimbursements.

Personal Mileage Reimbursement Personal mileage reimbursement can be easily manipulated. The travel and expense processor relies almost entirely on supervisory review and approval for validation. Employees may claim excess mileage or mileage for trips that never occurred.

- Analyze mileage reimbursements by employee for patterns. Develop a profile of what constitutes a "normal" profile for each employee. Examine variances from the norm, especially over time for further investigation.
- Analyze mileage reimbursements compared to timekeeping or other records. Verify mileage reimbursements occurred only on days that the employee worked.

Examination of Cash Patterns Certain transactions may always be paid in cash by specific employees. This could be a fraud indicator or ripe for abuse.

- Analyze cash transactions to develop a profile of the average traveler.
- Identify travelers that exclusively pay in cash for certain types of transactions. Compare to the average traveler profile.
- Perform Benford's Law Analysis on employee cash transactions. Extract outlier employee activity for further analysis.

Most Frequent Travelers Review the activity of the most frequent travelers.

- Determine whether the most frequent travelers are logical given job responsibilities.
- Examine expenditures for reasonableness.
- Examine destinations for reasonableness.

Executive Expenditures   Assess executive expenditures for reasonableness. The travel and expense processing department may be encouraged to reimburse executive expenditures without question. There have been numerous high-profile and embarrassing examples of corporate executives abusing the expense reimbursement process.

- Examine executive administrator expenses as part of the assessment. Are executives following policy? Are expenditures reasonable?
- Identification of expenditures just below thresholds requiring supporting documentation. Are there unusual patterns of activity for the company or individuals?
- Performance of Benford's Law Analysis on all expenditures. Benford's Law takes what is a normal expected (natural) distribution of digits (1–9) and compares it to actual distribution. Are any expenditures outside the expected and normal distribution curve? Analyze actual meal reimbursements. Actual meals reimbursements should create many combinations or payouts. Benford's Law will identify unusual patterns.
- Identification of hotel stays at non-preferred properties, unreasonable hotel rates, unreasonable hotel rate types (suite, upgraded rooms, etc.), and hotel rate packages (breakfast included).

Telecommunications

Company spending on telecommunications continues to increase with the growth of nontraditional work schedules, telecommuting, and the virtual work environment. Companies provide employees with mobile devices or reimburse a portion of personal mobile subscription plans. The opportunity here is to optimize the telecommunication spend according to actual experience and usage.

Telecommunication companies have no interest in informing a company that the enterprise-wide plan is suboptimal. Further, the company may not even have a telecommunications strategy, resulting in differing plans with multiple providers and no economies of scale. There are also third-party providers, who will monitor company usage and continuously optimize plans based on actual usage and share the savings. Companies can save upward of 50% of telecommunication expenditures through data analysis and optimization of plans.

Mobile

- Identify all telecommunication providers.
- Extract detailed telecommunication data usage for employees over prior 12 months.
- Analyze data and create a profile of the average user. Voice minutes, data usage, etc.
- Compare profile to telecommunication agreements. Determine whether the company is paying for excess capacity.
- If multiple providers are used, examine total usage when combined.
- Analyze data for unusual or added fees (e.g., late fees). Extract fees for investigation and potential refunds from provider.
- Based on evaluation, determine whether consolidation of plans would result in savings.
- Provide recommendations to the Supply Chain Organization for renegotiation or rebidding of plans.

Conference Calling Services Larger companies may use multiple conference calling service providers or may not have optimized conference calling plans. Many free conference calling services are now available. Competition in this space is increasing, and plan pricing is becoming competitive, especially if a company is armed with intelligence on its own usage.

- Identify all conference call service providers.
- Extract conference call usage data.
- Analyze data and determine whether use is aligned with current agreements. If the company is exceeding the monthly allotment, determine whether changing the plan is cheaper than paying overage per minute costs. If company usage is under the plan allotment, determine savings available by changing to plan with less minutes.
- Determine the last time conference calling plans were competitively bid. If greater than two years ago, consider whether rebidding is warranted.

Voice over Internet Protocol Plans Companies have been transitioning to Voice over Internet Protocol (VoIP) to increase productivity and the speed of connectivity, and to support virtual conferencing via Skype, WebEx, and other providers. The movement to VoIP is driving productivity and has massively reduced telecommunication costs. There is still an opportunity to determine whether the company's telecommunications organization has optimized agreements based on company usage experience and future needs.

Software Licenses

Software has proliferated with the movement to Software as a Service (SaaS). While enterprise licenses are becoming more common, individual software licenses are still common. The Supply Chain or IT organizations may not have the time or resources to analyze whether software licenses are actually being used. This is a great opportunity for internal audit to analyze the number of outstanding licensing and compare to actual usage.

- Identify all software licensed by the company.
- Request extracts from software providers for employee log in for software located in the cloud at the provider (vs. local copies).
- Analyze, by software, whether employees with licenses are using the software. Stratify by not used in the past 12 months, occasional use, and frequent users.
- Examine potential savings for licenses not used in the past 12 months. Individual licenses not used should be considered for cancellation. Individual licenses, depending on the provider, can run from $100 to $1,000 per license, delivering significant savings to the company.
- For enterprise-wide software agreements, analyze the actual usage of the software by employees. If 25% of employees are not using the product, the company should consider amending the agreement to reflect a smaller user base. This could result in significant savings.

Subscriptions

Subscriptions like software are often not utilized, leading to unnecessary expenditures. Subscriptions typically are evergreen agreements, where the company is charged on a recurring basis for the service without end. Individual, specialty subscriptions can be costly.

- Identify all company subscriptions for analysis. This can be achieved by extracting information from the vendor master file and/or accounts payable.
- Analyze enterprise-wide subscriptions to verify that the size of the user base reflects the actual employee population. If the subscription exceeds the user base, the agreement should be renegotiated.
- Analyze individual subscriptions. Determine whether there are multiple agreements for the same provider. Determine whether cost savings are available through consolidation to one, larger, subscription.
- Analyze whether the subscriptions are actually being utilized. Examine subscription recipients and determine whether it appears appropriate based on job role. Verify that subscriptions are being received by current employees (not terminated personnel).
- Analyze whether subscriptions are being sent to work or home addresses. If they are being sent to a home address, determine whether it is for personal use.
- Analyze the total cost of each subscription over the past five years. Providers will often increase subscription rates without notifying the company, and since the agreements are evergreen, no one notices.

Computer Hardware

Companies procure computer hardware to support company infrastructure and individual employee needs. Larger, more sophisticated companies may have defined choices for employee hardware (e.g., laptop) selection. Smaller and mid-sized companies may not prescribe a standard or preapproved option, preventing the company from achieving higher volume discounts. Companies may also purchase hardware from multiple providers, precluding realization of best pricing.

- Identify all providers of computer hardware by major category. In our example, we'll focus on laptop computers.

- Extract data on the types of computers purchased and unit price.
- Analyze and stratify computer purchases by type. Identify lowest, highest, and average unit price for each unit type. Calculate the total cost for each unit type if the lowest cost was paid. Analyze difference between actual total cost and total cost of lowest cost paid. This is the potential savings had a coordinated effort been made to purchase through one provider or by a central procurement agent.

Office Supplies

Office supply agreements usually contain larger discounts for higher volume items. Supply Chain Organizations may not verify that the highest volume items are receiving the deepest discounts. Agreements sometimes include a "market basket" of the company's top volume items. This market basket should be analyzed to verify optimal pricing.

- Identify all providers of office supplies. If more than one provider is used, the following analytics should be done for each and also combined by product type.
- Extract data from providers on items purchased over the past 12 months.
- Analyze purchases and identify the total volume for each item.
- Obtain pricing for each item and discount per agreement.
- Analyze to determine if the highest volume items are receiving the deepest discount.
- Analyze if similar but not identical types of office supplies are being purchased but not grouped together for discounting purposes. Identify total volume by item grouping (e.g., pens, staplers, and paper). If volume discounts are not being applied to the product grouping, recommend that the Supply Chain Organization adjust pricing with the supplier.
- If more than one provider is used, determine what the potential volume discount would be if the purchases were consolidated to one provider.

- Examine average cost per employee for office supplies, identify departments with significant variances from the average for further investigation. Office supplies are a frequent target of abuse and theft.
- Analyze data for items that shouldn't be purchased through office supply providers but may be available. Search by key word (MacBook, LCD, Bluetooth, etc.).
- Analyze data for shipping address. Verify that office supplies are shipped only to valid company addresses.

Shipping

Shipping charges can consist of everything from the mundane mailing of papers to the shipment of special care items. Companies often don't restrict which shipping providers can be used or how the shipment occurs.

- Identify all providers and request an extract of shipping data. This includes expenditures incurred for outgoing and incoming shipments/
- Analyze shipments by type (land, air, priority, next day, same day, overnight, etc.). Stratify data by timing of shipments. Calculate potential savings if same-day shipments were shipped overnight, next day, or two days later.
- If the company is using more than one provider (i.e., FedEx, DHL, UPS, USPS), analyze total activity for potential savings through consolidation to one provider or consolidation by shipment type to one provider (e.g., one provider provides all same day shipping). Working with the Supply Chain Organization, provide data for them to submit a Request for Information on rates from each provider if activity was consolidated.

Accounts Payable

Accounts payables, money owed to a company's vendors, is a rich source of potential cost savings and cost recovery. Duplicate payments may be made, discounts for paying by a certain date may be lost, and payments may be paid unnecessarily early.

Duplicate Payments

Objective: identify duplicate payments made.

- Extract data on payments made including vendor name, vendor number, payment amount, payment date, unique payment identifier (check #), invoice net amount, invoice creator identification, invoice date, invoice due date, invoice number, payment location, payment type (wire, check, etc.), and payment void date.
- Analyze data for payments for the same invoice amount, vendor name, and date. The key data point is invoice amount, as the payment could be for multiple invoices.
- Analyze payments for different vendors with similar names. I've seen numerous instances where a vendor will be set up with multiple variations of the same name, for instance, TrueTemper LTD, TrueTemper Co., TrueTemper Company, TrueTemp, True Temper Company, True Temper, etc. All of these create the potential for duplicate payments that go undetected.
- Analyze payments for different vendors with the same address. This is another potential for duplication of payment.

Vendor Credits

Objective: identify outstanding credits for inactive vendors.

- Query balances from the data extract by vendor name for credit balances.
- Evaluate age of credits.
- Request refunds for inactive vendors or greatly aged credits.

Payment Discounts

Objective: identify lost vendor payment discounts.

- Use the data extract from duplicate payments as well as an extract of the vendor master file.
- Extract vendors with payment discount terms and join to the accounts payable file on the common field vendor identification.

- Analyze payment date vs. due date to identify those vendors paid after the discount period.
- Calculate the total discount lost by vendor for the year.
- Recommend changes to the payment schedule for those vendors with lost discounts in order to realize future discounts. Recommend that the Supply Chain Organization approach the vendors to negotiate refunds for some of the discounts already lost.

Cash Flow (Commercial Enterprise)

Objective: optimize cash flow related to payments.

- Using the original data extract, create and calculate a new field, number of days to pay by vendor, by comparing invoice due date to the actual date payment was made.
- Analyze the difference between the number of days to pay and the payment terms (10, 30, 45 days) by vendor for all payments.
- The difference represents underutilized cash flow. Consider adding an interest rate factor to calculate the potential impact to cash flow. By optimizing the timing of payments, the company can improve its cash flow overall, freeing up cash for other uses or internal funding.

Detecting Fraud

Accounts payable can present fraud risk. There are some simple analytic techniques to monitor for fraud prevention and detection. The economist Dr. Hal Varian pioneered the idea that Benford's Law could be used to detect fraud. Essentially, Benford's Law takes what is a normal expected (natural) distribution of digits (1–9) and compares it to actual distribution. If someone is committing fraud, the idea is that they will be unable to distribute their payment amounts in a manner that is not uniform. For example, they may repeat digits more frequently than expected (39.99, 39.98, 39.97, etc.).

- Using the original extract, perform a Benford's Law Analysis on the data. Benford's Law Analysis is available in most analytic software packages. If a vendor or employee is manipulating payments, Benford's Law will identify aberrations against what a normal payments distribution would look like. Extract unexpected variances for further investigation.

- Benford Analysis will also identify payment splitting, whereby employees will split the payment to a vendor to avoid exceeding authorization requirements. For example, if a company requires additional approval for payments above $10,000, someone avoiding this threshold may submit two requests for vendor payments to stay below the threshold and avoid the additional scrutiny. Often employees will simply divide the payment amount in half. This occurs at virtually every company.

- Using the original payments, extract join the data with an extract of employee addresses. Analyze and identify payments sent to employee addresses. Perform additional analysis for unexpected outcomes.

There are many additional potential areas for analysis. As we discussed at the beginning of the chapter, the only limitation is your imagination! Some additional areas that I've found to be fruitful include Inventory, Petty Cash, Payroll, Corporate Credit Cards, Accounts Receivable, Overtime Pay, Benefits Programs, Consultants, Computer Hardware, Intellectual Property and Licensing, Construction, and Major Vendor Agreements.

Chapter Recap

Data analytics offer a quick way to deliver value for customers. The use of analytics can identify cost savings and revenue recoveries, turning internal audit into a profit center. Every process has data associated with it. Internal audit is in a unique position to provide insights for customers by incorporating data analytics as part of each audit and special project. Established and repeatable data analytic scripts support continuous monitoring for the customer and frees-up internal audit time to evaluate other risks. Robotic Process Automation will accelerate the ability to run multiple and continuous data analytic monitoring scripts. Partnering with customers to identify data to monitor, adds value.

Bibliography

The National Council for Excellence in Critical Thinking. https://en.wikipedia.org/wiki/Benford%27s_law.

Index